Contents

Praise for *Avoiding Worker Lawsuits and Litigation*

"*Avoiding Worker Lawsuits and Litigation* is an approachable and practical text for any human resource department but a lifeline for the small business owner who is trying to do it all themselves. Get back to running the business you love and let this essential guide help you negotiate away from problems every business wants to avoid."

—**Dr. Ron and Linda Ruthruff**, Nonprofit leader for 30 years and Founding Director of Street Bean Espresso

"Ray Sugarman's *Avoiding Worker Lawsuits and Litigation* provides essential information for business owners and senior staff. Written in a practical, easy to understand manner, Sugarman explains the laws without using legal jargon. It is a practical primer for anyone handling human resource responsibilities. This book is the tool small businesses and nonprofits need to avoid mistakes and costly lawsuits, as well as to know how to provide clear expectations for employees and maintain a hospitable working environment."

—**Dawn Trudeau**, Co-Owner of WNBA Seattle Storm, Force 10 Enterprises, and Force 10 Sports Management

"Small non-profits cannot afford to have a personnel director or human resources department. As a result, often executives of these non-profits make inadvertent mistakes in personnel policy and in managing and supervising staff. To avoid this situation, which can put a non-profit into existential crisis, grab this book and read it. For small non-profits, it is a necessary guide for ensuring that your workplace follows the law, honors its workers with respect, and insulates itself from malicious behavior."

—**John Burbank**, MPA, Executive Director of Economic Opportunity Institute

"This is the desktop HR guide you need! Ray provides a crash course in full cycle HR management for HR teams, business and employees. If more companies put these basic principles into action, employees would be better connected and fulfilled in their work. Start at the front with your workplace culture in mind and you won't regret it—neither will your employees!"

—**Bobby Humes**, MSHR, Director of City of Seattle Department of Human Resources

"*Avoiding Worker Lawsuits and Litigation* is essential reading for all entrepreneurs and business owners. If you plan to hire employees or work with contractors, this book can help you maintain good working relationships and avoid costly mistakes. Well written and concise, and full of practical tips and legal insights, you'll do well to read it repeatedly."

—**Mushka Rohani**, MBA, Executive Director of Human Resources at Edmonds Community College

AVOIDING WORKER LAWSUITS AND LITIGATION

A GUIDE FOR HR-LESS EMPLOYERS

RAY SUGARMAN

Novo Dia
MEDIA

Published by Novo Dia Media, Seattle, Washington

1st Edition 2020

ISBN: 978-1-7349336-0-4 (Paperback)
ISBN: 978-1-7349336-2-8 (Hardback)
ISBN: 978-1-7349336-1-1 (Ebook)

Library of Congress Control Number: 2020937334

Edited by Mikel Benton
Book design by DesignForBooks.com

Printed in the U.S.A

DISCLAIMER

This publication is intended for general information purposes only. It does not constitute legal advice. Readers should consult with knowledgeable legal counsel to determine how applicable laws apply to specific facts and situations. This publication is based on the most current information at the time it was written. It is possible that the laws or other circumstances may have changed since publication. Readers should contact their own legal counsel to discuss any actions they may be considering as a result of reading this publication.

Why You Need This Book

Nearly one-fifth of small businesses that go bankrupt, do so as a result of lawsuits, according to a recent poll.[1]

Letting inappropriate action in the hiring process or workplace go unchecked can lead to costly lawsuits and time-consuming litigation. A company's productivity, finances, reputation, and ability to attract talent can all suffer. One employee lawsuit may also be followed by other employee lawsuits. Some mistakes could even bankrupt your business!

Large companies protect themselves by having human resource (HR) departments staffed with employee relation advisors and legal consultants. But what if you are a small business without an HR department? If you hire employees, and you are not familiar with labor law and don't understand your duties and responsibilities to your workers, you may violate their rights unknowingly.

Typically, small business owners hire employees because they have a vision they want to cultivate, not because they are highly skilled labor law experts waiting to address internal personnel issues. And that's why I wrote this book. This book provides critical information, in the most concise way possible, to help small business owners and entrepreneurs avoid common employee problems. Some topics deserve a deeper dive into the nuances of the law and may require additional research or consulting a legal expert. But this book will offer a starting point and give you the general information you need to avoid worker lawsuits. In this guide, you'll learn

- ✓ the essential legal landscape,
- ✓ what actions create legal exposure,
- ✓ practical workplace policies and procedures,
- ✓ how to compile proper documentation,
- ✓ how to respond to complex situations with creative solutions, and
- ✓ when outside assistance is necessary.

Employee Onboarding

1

"What a worker experiences during their first days and weeks at a new job will impact their entire experience. Too often, poor onboarding can cut that experience short. In fact, employees often decide within their first 30 days whether they are going to stick with a company."[2]

Protections are extended to workers well before they even begin working for an employer. State and federal anti-discrimination laws protect individuals' rights "to obtain *and* hold employment." This means that the law protects not only current employees from discrimination in the workplace, but it also protects all individuals applying for employment. As such, employers need to be diligent in establishing policies and procedures that not only ensure that current employees' rights are not violated, but that applicants' rights aren't as well. This requires assessing the entire hiring process—including the job advertisement, the entire interview process, and the offer—and all employment thereafter. Employers need to begin by ensuring that they have legally sound job descriptions, nondiscriminatory job advertisements, and thought-out interview processes, including specific interview questions.

Employers need to issue any intended covenants at the onset of employment . . .

Additionally, when onboarding new hires, this is the time to consider whether you will want them to be held to any *post-employment agreements*. Post-employment agreements (such as noncompetes, nonsolicits, and nondisclosure agreements), more commonly referred to as *restrictive covenants*, are employee contracts that prohibit employees from engaging in specific actions once their employment has concluded. They are intended to protect employers by preventing former employees from using particular information gained in their employment for the benefit of other employers. Employers need to issue any intended covenants at the onset of employment or risk having to offer additional consideration to employees later to get them to sign the agreements, such as pay them more money.

Job Description Requirements

Job descriptions may become the crux of employee lawsuits, as illustrated by Snead v. Florida Agricultural and Mechanical University Board of Trustees, *in which the vague job description was the determining evidence held against the* *employer. In this case, the employee's job description did not state that twelve-hour shifts might be required, and when his employer changed his standard working shifts from eight hours per day to twelve, the plaintiff, Stanley Snead, began experiencing high blood pressure. "After the employee's doctor identified the twelve-hour shifts as the culprit, the employee requested to work shorter shifts. The employer refused, and the employee retired," according to David Miklas, a labor and employment attorney in Port St. Lucie, Florida. Mr. Snead filed suit against his employer, the Florida Agricultural and Mechanical University, for violating his ADA rights. The jury agreed and awarded him $142,268 for lost wages and benefits, and $108,810 for mental and emotional anguish. On appeal, the Eleventh Circuit affirmed the jury's ruling, finding that the former employee could perform the essential functions of the position as described in the job description. However, it did not mention twelve-hour shifts, and thus, held the employer to be at fault.*[3]

A job description is the formal summary of an employee's responsibilities associated with a particular position. Job descriptions need to be more than just a general and broad outline of the workplace expectations. They need to be tailored to the responsibilities of each specific position. Employer-friendly job descriptions usually state certain duties in broad or general language, as to allow some flexibility for the employer to assign an array of tasks, but are explicit in stating any specific unique tasks, requirements, and qualifications that are necessary or desired for the position. These requirements and qualifications should be based on a job analysis as to what exactly each position entails.

It is important to have a well written job description for many reasons that go beyond simply being able to post a job advertisement that accurately describes the position.

Benefits of a Well Written Job Description

Accurately written job descriptions assist employers for recruiting purposes, but they can also assist

- managing work-task performance,
- determining proper compensation,
- acting as one of the most critical documents when engaging in the ADA accommodation process, and
- reinserting an employee back into the workforce after returning from extended leave.

Elements of a Job Description

In addition to the title of the position, a well-written job description should include, at a minimum, (a) the classification, which speaks to the FLSA considerations, (b) essential duties, (c) qualifications (minimum and desirable), (d) physical requirements, (e) disclaimers, and (f) any additional considerations expected of the position.

(a) The **classification** section needs to very clearly and explicitly state whether the position is at will, and whether it is exempt or nonexempt. Notifying employees that their employment is at will is relaying the contractual relationship with the employer, that employees may be dismissed for any reason or no reason at all (as long as it is not discriminatory). Stating whether a position is exempt or not notifies employees or potential applicants whether the position is protected under federal law overtime provisions. Additionally, the classification needs to state whether the position is full time or part time.

(b) The **duties** section needs to clearly spell out what the essential duties of the position are. Being sure to include any and all potential functions that may be required of the position is critical. The essential functions as listed in the job description are what will be assessed when determining the parameters of an ADA accommodation for a disability or for a religious accommodation. Additionally, if the situation ever arises of finding a suitable analogous position for an employee returning from leave, it is the essential functions of the positions that will be determinative. In this area, it is worth taking extra time to be as specific and inclusive as possible. In the duties section, notice should be given that reserves the employer's right to add additional duties not listed. A simple example of a statement reserving such a right might read, "and other duties as assigned." This grants some discretionary authority for the employer to assign tasks not explicitly mentioned in the duties section.

(c) The **qualifications** section usually consists of a listing of the minimum qualifications and desirable qualifications for a position. At the very least, nearly every job description needs to include the minimum requirements that any applicant must meet in order to be considered for a position. This may include requirements as to educational level, professional certifications, specific technical skills and expertise, or a minimal amount of prior work experience. It is important for an employer to clearly assess what qualifications the potential employee must absolutely possess and distinguish those from qualifications that are merely desired.

The employer may use the minimum qualifications section of a job description to act as a filter from overly burdensome numbers of applicants. At the same time, minimum qualifications can be used as a tool for employers to make sure their employees maintain certain industry standards and professional certifications.

As mentioned earlier, every applicant is a potential plaintiff. As such, it is a best practice to avoid allowing applicants who do not possess the minimum qualifications to proceed in the hiring process. Rejecting applicants who do meet all minimum qualifications without additional reasons is an invitation for a lawsuit. It is the additional "desirable qualifications" that allow employers to have more discretion and flexibility in whom they offer a position to.

(d) Any **physical requirements** for a position need to be clearly stated in the job description. An employer should look through the essential functions of the position and determine what physical requirements or skills are required to carry out these functions. It is a best practice to mention even mundane activities that the position may require that must be done for an extended period. This may include long periods of standing, sitting, typing, repetitive motions, or any lifting requirements.

Job descriptions should mention any mundane activities the position may require that must be done for an extended period.

(e) Each job description should include a **disclaimer**. This disclaimer should (1) explicitly grant the employer the right to modify the job description at their discretion, and (2) allow for additional duties and responsibilities not listed to be included. One disclaimer can satisfy both of these points, such as stating, "The duties and responsibilities set forth above are not intended to be an exhaustive list; rather, the employer reserves the right to add additional tasks that may be deemed necessary from time to time." A disclaimer such as this can be used to support any minor changes in duties and responsibilities of a position, but it likely would not be sufficient to support any substantial or unique deviations from the job description.

(f) **Other considerations**: It is always best practice to mention in the job description any other foreseeable or unordinary conditions the position may require. These additional considerations should include the general working hours (i.e., day-shift, swing-shift, graveyard-shift), any required travel, required trainings, certification upkeep, safety considerations, etc.

Maintenance: Job descriptions need to be assessed and updated on a regular basis. Outdated or inaccurate job descriptions can create liability exposure for almost any employer. It is recommended that employers review and update their job descriptions semi-annually and every time the employer is hiring for the position.

TIPS FOR DRAFTING JOB DESCRIPTIONS

1. The job description should state whether the position is at will, exempt, or full time.
2. The essential duties need to include any and all potential functions that may be required of the position.
3. Include a statement allowing the employer to assign additional duties not explicitly stated, such as including "and other duties as assigned."
4. Do not allow applicants not meeting the minimum qualifications to proceed in the interview process; a section listing "desirable qualifications" is the opportunity to include additional sought-after qualifications while still maintaining flexibility selecting an applicant.

5. Include any foreseeable or unordinary conditions the position may require, such as trainings, odd work shifts, whether travel will be required, certification upkeep, etc.
6. Periodically review job descriptions on a bi-annual basis and each time the position is advertised for hiring.

Employee Inquiries and Interviews

In response to a 2012 EEOC complaint alleging discrimination, Alliant Techsystems, one of the largest aerospace and defense manufacturers in the country, settled for $100,000. The complaint alleged that Alliant had failed to hire an African American woman because of her race, based on comments and statements made to her during the hiring process. A recruiter for the tech company advised the applicant to take out her braids for her interviews, in order to appear more professional, to which the applicant complied. After several interviews, without her braids in, she was told by the recruiter that the company wanted to hire her, however, she needed to meet with the IT director. For this interaction, the applicant had braids back in her hair, and the following day, she was informed that the company would not be *hiring her. Shortly thereafter, the company hired a white male for the position.*[4]

As mentioned, the law protects not only individuals already employed from discrimination but also those seeking to gain employment. This means that every applicant is a potential plaintiff. So following best practices when conducting interviews is very important for every employer, especially when they are going to interact with so many individuals, who also likely span the gamut regarding sensitivity to their rights and the questions asked of them.

Every applicant is a potential plaintiff.

Once an employer becomes aware of the legal minefield a simple employee interview can be, it can become a stressful, confusing, and anxiety-ridden situation. Even some HR specialists become intimidated by the difficulties of navigating interviews. However, it doesn't need to be this way. With an overview of what types of inquiries to avoid, an understanding of how to plan for interviews, and samples of commonly asked illegal questions, along with alternative model questions that still get the desired information, any employer can feel confident going into any interview that they won't overstep and create liability exposure by asking an inappropriate question. The interview can then be worry-free and focused on what is important—whether the candidate will be a good fit.

The law protects all potential employees from discrimination.

Whom the Law Protects and from What

As an employer, it is important to know whom the law protects and from what exactly. The law protects all potential employees from discrimination. As stated earlier, this means that all applicants are potential plaintiffs to an employer. The law recognizes discrimination based on certain protected classifications. These protected classifications may include

- age,
- race,
- national origin,
- citizenship,
- gender,
- marital status,
- sexual orientation,
- pregnancy status,
- disabilities,
- military discharge status,
- genetic information, and
- arrest and conviction record.

This means that inquiries into these categories may potentially be illegal. Local and state municipalities may have protections more expansive than the federal protections.

> The law's protections against discrimination are applicable to all questions asked throughout the hiring process, not just the interview.

IMPORTANT: Every employer should recognize that the law's protections against discrimination are applicable to all questions asked throughout the hiring process. The law presumes that all inquiries made throughout the hiring process will be taken into consideration for the position. This means two things for an employer. First, all inquiries made can potentially be recognized as illegal inquiries, whether formal or informal, written or oral, in or outside the official interview, by the employer or another potential decision-maker. Second, this also includes interview notes. As such, be sure to not write any identifying information on the job applications or in interview notes, such as the applicants' gender, race, age, etc.

Common Legal Traps

As the law in the employment sector has rapidly grown over the recent years, a series of protections has emerged or expanded and has created common legal traps for employers in the interview process. These growing legal traps include questions regarding (a) access to social media, (b) family, (c) arrest or conviction history, and (d) political ideology.

(a) **Social Media** – A new and rapidly growing area of employment law has been in regard to social media. The law has been attempting to find the balance between employers' interest in being able to view or access employees' social media activity and employees' rights to privacy and freedom of speech. In some states, laws have been enacted that protect applicants and employees from being required to disclose social media log-in information, show an employer private accounts, accept employers' friend requests, or make private accounts public.[5]

As a best practice, employers should have explicit policies and procedures in place stating that internet searches of applicants are only conducted by trained HR professionals, are only for publicly available social media, are done in a consistent manner, that records are kept of searches via screen shots and search logs, and only redacted results are provided to decision makers. This will be discussed further in a following section.

Additional information on addressing social media issues is available in the chapter Employee Misconduct, under "Off-Duty Behavior and Social Media" (page 142).

(b) **Family** – As impersonal as it may seem, employers should steer clear of questions regarding candidates' families, especially in interviews. Developing law has created protections for discriminating against workers based on their families. Additionally, it is unpredictable when a seemingly innocent question regarding children can reveal or lead into a conversation regarding race, disability, national origin, or some other protected class. As such, employers should not ask about a candidate's spouse, spouse's gender, spouse's employment or salary, children, pregnancy, child-care arrangements, or dependents. While there are legitimate reasons an employer may want to inquire into some of these categories as they may be relevant to other aspects of the job, examples of alternative and carefully crafted questions that can help get the same information the employer truly needs without violating an applicant's rights are provided in the next section.

(c) **Arrests and Convictions** – This is another relatively new and rapidly growing area of employment law. Employers should review applicable state and local laws restricting inquiries into arrests or conviction history of applicants, as many municipalities have enacted laws on this topic in recent years.

Employers should steer clear of questions regarding candidates' families.

Federal Protections

Currently, some federal laws already protect applicants with criminal records. Under the Equal Employment Opportunity Commission (EEOC) and the Fair Credit Reporting Act (FCRA), an employer seeking to have an applicant's background check conducted by a third party must first obtain the applicant's written consent and take other steps before rejecting an applicant based on the background check's results.

Additionally, given the disparate impact that the criminal justice system has had on people of color, the EEOC has advised employers against having blanket policies excluding all applicants with criminal records, as this practice likely will result in disproportionately excluding African Americans and Latinos, which may constitute discrimination.[6]

State and Local Protections

Even more restrictive than federal law are the various state and local government laws protecting applicants and the use of their criminal records in the hiring process. A number of states have enacted laws spanning the spectrum on various types of restrictions and conditions that employers may ask applicants about their criminal records. Some laws prohibit employers from asking applicants about arrests that did not lead to convictions or prohibit employers from asking about convictions, unless they relate directly to the job. Other laws take a more holistic approach and require employers who consider convictions to take into consideration additional information about a conviction, such as how serious the crime was and whether the applicant took part in any rehabilitation efforts. What is likely the most protective of applicants' criminal histories is happening in a growing number of states and cities, such as Seattle, Washington, with the enactment of "ban the box" laws. These protections prohibit employers from asking applicants about their criminal histories until after they've been interviewed or have received conditional offers of employment. As such, questions about criminal history likely won't show up on job applications in areas where these protections are in place.

Do not ask about criminal history in the interview.

Even for employers who are not restricted by law from asking about applicants' criminal histories on their job applications, the best practice is to never bring it up in an interview, nor should the results of a criminal background check ever be discussed in an interview. It is best to wait until after a conditional offer has been made. This also helps keep more qualified candidates in the pipeline.

To learn more about the applicable laws regarding an employer's use of arrest and conviction records, see "Additional Information" at the end of the chapter (page 36).[7]

(d) **Political Ideology** – Generally, an employer should not ask questions about an applicant's political affiliation. Political ideology, in some jurisdictions, is a protected classification. This is important for employers to be aware of, especially in today's social climate in which conversations and opinions regarding political affiliation are more common and less passive.

Disability and Accommodation Questions

The Americans with Disabilities Act (ADA) prohibits discrimination in the workplace based on a person's disabilities. As such, the best practice is simple: do not discuss or ask applicants about disabilities or accommodations during interviews. Do not even mention "disability." Do not ask whether applicants have any disabilities. And do not ask applicants whether they need any reasonable accommodations during the interview.

Do not discuss or ask an applicant about disabilities or accommodations during the interview.

What an employer can discuss and ask about are the essential functions of the position. An employer can describe the essential functions of the position being sought and ask whether applicants can perform those tasks "with or without" reasonable accommodations. Additionally, the employer may ask applicants to demonstrate or explain how they will perform a position's essential functions, when applicable (for a deeper dive into inquiries into disabilities during interviews, see "Additional Information" at the end of the chapter on page 36).[8]

There are three exceptions to the "no disability discussion rule":

Laws to Know

1. An employer can inquire, indirectly, about disabilities, when asking whether applicants need reasonable accommodation *to assist in the hiring process*, e.g., assistance filling out applications.

2. An employer can ask whether applicants need reasonable accommodations to perform essential functions *and* what types of accommodations would be needed. This is only allowed to be asked *when the employer has a reasonable belief* that applicants will need accommodations to perform essential functions of a job.

   "Reasonable belief" may be satisfied in situations involving applicants' having (i) obvious disabilities, e.g., leg cast; (ii) when applicants voluntarily disclose hidden disabilities, e.g., diabetes; or (iii) when applicants voluntarily disclose that they will need reasonable accommodations for the position (however, this does not give an invitation for the interviewer to ask more questions or fish for additional information).

3. Employers are allowed to provide *conditional offers of employment and explore reasonable accommodation* issues with employees, but only after conditional offers have been made. However, employers must be mindful that if they provide reasonable accommodations, they cannot retract those offers for any reason.[9]

Tips for the Interview Process

Although conducting an interview while navigating anti-discrimination legislation can feel like a daunting task, it doesn't have to complicate the interview process.

1. **Know what information you want to ascertain prior to the interview.** You can make simple adjustments to questions that may be inappropriate, and be at ease and sail through the questions and interview learning what you really want to know (the candidate's suitability for the position) without getting off track and into irrelevant personal information (that you don't need to make a decision).

2. **Control the conversation, especially around sensitive topics.** Even if you're in a comfortable setting asking job interview questions, make sure that you don't let the discussion turn into an impromptu chat session. This could easily happen, especially when you take job applicants out for lunch or dinner. Even the most innocuous job interview questions may be illegal.

3. **Avoid questions that allude to protected classifications.** While you can rephrase a question to get the information you're after without demonstrating bias, keep in mind that questions that might allude to any protected classifications should be avoided. For example, asking applicants their high school or college graduation year will inevitably give you a general estimate as to the applicants' ages.

4. **Write out what specific information** you want to know about the applicants, and then write out questions that directly address that point. The value of planning ahead for interviews is that you can have a plan for how the interview will go and the specific questions that you will ask. Interviewers will likely not be able to think of appropriate questions on

the spot that solicit the information they need without overstepping and inadvertently asking something inappropriate.

5. **Review the questions you want to ask.** It is always best practice to write out the questions you want to ask, and then go over them again, or perhaps have another colleague go over them and check for any potential illegal inquiries. It is also important to note questions which may provide specific information on one of the protected classes, so that you are prepared to not let applicants go on with their responses and potentially relay personal information. Be sure to review and reword any questions that could potentially create liability if they are shown to demonstrate a bias toward a protected class.

Below are common ways employers inadvertently overstep in interviews with applicants, along with recommendations to address and avoid them, including some alternative questions compiled by HR and employment law experts through the NCVO.[10]

1. *Place of Birth, Ethnicity, or Religion* – Employers should avoid all questions regarding an applicant's birthplace, background, ethnicity, and religious affiliation.

- A seemingly innocent question such as, "Where are you from?" or, "Where were you born?" should be avoided. On this topic, the only question that should be asked is whether the applicant is eligible to work in the country.
- Although applicants may voluntarily disclose their ethnicity on their job applications, this should not be brought up or discussed in the interview.
- If an applicant has an unusual name, interviewers should not ask about it, as this may seem to be an inquiry into that individual's national origin or even religious affiliation.
- Interviewers should not ask about the applicant's native language but can ask if the applicant is fluent in any other languages, if it is relevant to the position.
- Although an employer may want to know what religious obligations applicants have that may influence their work schedules, they should not ask what applicants' religious practices are but, instead, can ask if they have any obligations that may affect their schedules.

2. *Marital Status, Children or Sexual Preference* – Although questions regarding an applicant's family may be an innocent attempt to seem less impersonal as an employer and to show interest in the applicant beyond the job setting, these questions should be avoided in an interview.

   - Employers should not ask applicants about their families, whether they plan to have one, any questions regarding pregnancy, whether they plan take time off for pregnancy, or about their childcare arrangements.
   - Additionally, employers should steer clear of questions about applicants' spouses, marital status, and sexual orientation.
   - Instead of asking whether applicants have or plan to have children, an interviewer can ask if they are available to work overtime on occasions or travel for work, or inquire into their availability during certain periods of time. For example, an interviewer might ask, "Are you going to be available for the next three/six/twelve months?"
   - Instead of asking about an applicant's intentions for maternity leave, an employer

should ask what the applicant's long-term career goals are.

- Employers should not ask about the number of children the applicant has or about childcare arrangements. Instead, an employer should relay that the position may require occasional overtime and ask whether that might be a problem, and what days or hours the employee would be available.
- Asking whether an applicant's name is a maiden name can reasonably be construed as asking about marital status and should be avoided. An alternative to that question could be whether the applicant has any references or qualifications under another name.

3. *Gender or Age* – Employers should not ask questions regarding applicants' age or gender. Although employers may have an interest in knowing whether applicants can carry out the duties of their positions, no reference should be made that age or gender may affect their abilities.

- Employers should not ask about an applicants' ability to work with the opposite gender, but may ask about their communication and management styles, or if they foresee any issues working in their workgroups.

- Generally, the only questions regarding age should be whether or not the applicant meets the minimum age requirements for the position.
- Additionally, employers should not make any inferences about retirement based on the applicant's age or ask when an applicant intends on retiring. Instead, an employer may ask what long-term career goals the applicant has.

4. *Location* – Employers should not ask applicants about their commuting times, whether they have vehicles or take public transportation, or whether they live nearby. This is an easy topic of discussion to wander into without an established interview game plan. Even asking what neighborhood an applicant lives in can expose the employer to a discrimination lawsuit, especially if the area is heavily populated by an ethnic group.
   - Instead of asking how far applicants' commutes will be, ask if they are able to get to work by the relative start time.

5. *Disability or Illness* – As mentioned in the prior section, the Americans with Disabilities Act prohibits discrimination based on a person's disabilities. As such, all questions of disability and illness generally should be avoided, unless one of the three exceptions apply. For further information, see the Disability and Accommodations Questions section (page 20).

    - Although it is reasonable to inquire into any extended gaps of work in an applicant's resume, questions directly about illnesses or health conditions should be avoided.

    - An employer should not ask how often applicants plan to call in sick, but can ask how many unscheduled days of work they missed the past year in their prior employment.

6. *Lifestyle Choices* – Employers should avoid questions regarding applicants' lifestyle choices or what applicants do outside of work if it has no bearing on suitability for the position. Common examples of these types of inquiries include questions regarding any clubs or organizations they belong to (unless related to the position), political affiliations,

being a member of the military reserves, criminal records, and social media.

- Although an employer has an interest in knowing what other obligations or scheduling constraints applicants have that may affect their availability or performance, it is best practice to simply ask if they are able to commit to the position.

7. *Height or Weight* – It is also best to avoid questions about applicants' weight or height, unless there are certain minimum or maximum requirements for the position.

   - Instead of asking how tall/short they are, employers should ask whether they are able to accomplish certain functions of the position, e.g., whether they are able to reach the high shelf that materials are placed on.

   - Additionally, interviewers should not ask about applicants' weight or physical fitness, but instead can ask whether applicants can carry out certain functions of the position in which weight or strength may be relevant, such as whether they are able to carry materials weighing up to 45 pounds.

How to Protect Your Customer Base and Proprietary Business Information

> *WeWork, an international company providing rental shared space, used noncompete agreements with nearly 3,300 of its employees, and after a recent settlement with the attorney generals for New York and Illinois, almost half were invalidated entirely and only the noncompetes for 100 executive-level employees remained fully in intact.*[11]

Employers have a legitimate interest in protecting their customer bases and proprietary business information. To protect these interests, employers commonly use *restrictive covenants*, also known as *post-employment agreements*. Restrictive covenants are employer contracts signed by employees in which they agree not to engage in specific actions once their employment with the employer has concluded. These restrictions are intended to protect employers by preventing former employees from using particular information gained in their employment for the benefit of their new jobs.

It is important for employers seeking to use restrictive covenants to be sure that they are being carefully and meticulously drafted. It is recommended that they consult with an employment attorney when drafting these policies, as predictability of enforceability is highly uncertain and may be influenced by recent case decisions.

Common restrictive agreements include noncompete, non-solicit, and nondisclosure covenants. Although restrictive covenants may be one of the only tools reasonably available to protect an employer's interests from former employees, they are highly scrutinized by the courts, rarely in favor of the employer. As such, it is important for employers seeking to use restrictive covenants to be sure that they are being carefully and meticulously drafted. It is recommended that they consult with an employment attorney when drafting these policies, as predictability of enforceability is highly uncertain and may be influenced by recent case decisions.

> *Courts highly scrutinize post-employment restrictive covenants.*

Courts highly scrutinize post-employment restrictive covenants because of the perceived disparity in bargaining power between the employer and the employee. Although employers have a right to protect their business interests, courts recognize and emphasize the employees' right to earn a living. This right is usually analyzed in the context of limiting society's privilege to free competition and restraints on and against trade. Contracts restraining trade and competition generally are recognized as being against public policy and are therefore unenforceable.

Laws to Know

Legal Standard for Restrictive Covenants

The laws vary widely from state to state regarding the enforceability of restrictive covenants. Some states assess the legitimacy of restrictive covenants based on common law precedent, while other states and local governments have their own specific statutes in place.

Most courts adopting the common law standard try to balance the competing interests between employers' need for protection and society's privilege to free trade and competition, and will only enforce a restrictive covenant if it is determined to be reasonable. To be reasonable, it must not be any more restrictive than necessary to protect the employer's interest. Courts will determine reasonableness by assessing three factors:

1. time (duration of the covenant),
2. geographical scope (the territorial effect on the industry and reasonableness of the geographical size), and,
3. scope of the employer's business interests sought to be protected weighed against the effect on the employee.

Each of these factors must be strictly limited in scope for the restrictive covenant to be reasonable and, thus, enforceable.

States with their own statutes span the spectrum regarding their hostility toward restrictive covenants, from California, which is significantly employee-friendly with restrictions that generally prohibit noncompete agreements entirely, to employer-friendly states such as Michigan, which explicitly allows for noncompete agreements.[12] For more information on various state restrictions on restrictive covenants, please see "Additional Information" on page 36.

Various Common Restrictive Covenants

Each type of restrictive covenant protects a different interest of the employer, and it is the specific interest of the employer that is assessed against the effect on the employee. As such, one boiler-plate clause for all restrictive covenants will likely not be sufficient to protect all the interests of the employer. Each covenant should be crafted based on specific, relevant facts and consider the actual and practical impact it will have on the employee. Additionally, breaking these various covenants into separate clauses in the contract creates greater protection of the employer's interests. By separating the clauses, the court may still enforce portions of the contract held to be reasonable in the event that it refuses to enforce one of the clauses.

Each covenant should . . . consider the actual and practical impact it will have on the employee.

Common restrictive covenants include:

(a) *Non-Compete Clauses* – prevent a separating employee from competing with the employer and/or from working for a competitor of the employer within a limited geographical scope, for a period of time.

(b) *Non-Solicitation Clauses* – preclude an employee from soliciting clients of the employer for a period of time after separation.

(c) *Non-Recruitment Clauses* – prohibit an employee from recruiting employees of the employer for a period of time after separation.

(d) *Confidentiality Clauses/Nondisclosure Agreements* – limit the use of an employer's confidential or proprietary information by an employee during and after the period of employment.

TIPS FOR CRAFTING AND ADMINISTERING RESTRICTIVE COVENANTS

1. Prior to making an employment offer, assess whether there are any employer interests needing protection and what the best tool to protect that interest is, e.g., non-solicit, non-compete, etc.

2. Do not use boiler-plate covenants. They should be crafted specifically based on actual needs and relevant facts.

3. Limit the duration and geographical scope of covenants as narrowly as necessary.

4. Draft the covenants independently, in separate clauses.

Additional Information

- State Laws Restricting an Employer's Use of Arrest and Conviction Records – **Nolo, Legal Encyclopedia**, "State Laws on Use of Arrests and Convictions in Employment," https://www.nolo.com/legal-encyclopedia/state-laws-use-arrests-convictions-employment.html.
- Employer Responsibilities Under the ADA – **U.S. Equal Employment Opportunity Commission**, "The ADA: Your Responsibilities as an Employer," https://www.eeoc.gov/facts/ada17.html.
- Employer Interview Questions Related to the ADA – **EEOC**, "Enforcement Guidance: Preemployment Disability-Related Questions and Medical Examinations," https://www.eeoc.gov/policy/docs/preemp.html.
- Fifty-State Survey Detailing the Laws of Restrictive Covenants – **Fox Rothschild**, "National Survey on Restrictive Covenants," July 2017, https://www.foxrothschild.com/publications/national-survey-on-restrictive-covenants-in-employment/.

Wage and Hour Laws You Need to Know

2

The number of FLSA lawsuits has sharply risen each year, from the 1,558 lawsuits filed against employers in 1997[13] *to 7,694 FLSA suits filed in 2018.*[14]

Employer Responsibilities

Employees are protected by federal, state, and local laws. Violating these laws and protections can land you in court or worse. The federal government pursued thousands of employee wage and hour cases in 2019, resulting in a record of over $322 million in back wages owed to workers.[15] Other penalties employers may incur include significantly high fines, expensive legal fees (yours and the employees', which can be more expensive than the violations themselves), lost time, mandatory trainings, and invitations for more lawsuits.

At the federal level, there are many Department of Labor (DOL) laws that employers must be in compliance with. These laws touch on many aspects of employment, such as wage and hours, workplace safety, and family medical leave. One of the largest bodies of federal law controlling the wage and hour legal landscape is the Fair Labor Standards Act (FLSA).

The FLSA establishes various employee protections for matters concerning wage and hour issues, such as setting the federal minimum wage, overtime pay eligibility, recordkeeping, and child labor standards. These protections affect workers in the private sector and most of the public sector. While the FLSA sets the minimal labor protections granted to employees, employers should also review applicable state laws, as state or local ordinances may grant greater protections to employees than the FLSA. For example, a number of states set the minimum wage higher than that set by the FLSA.

Common Violations to Avoid

FLSA violations are a common reason for lawsuits against employers. Oftentimes, employers are committing violations unintentionally, but ignorance is not a defense for an employer.

COMMON VIOLATIONS

Employers should become familiar with the FLSA and some of the common violations:

1. Misclassifying employees
2. Overlooking off-the-clock work
3. Failing to pay unauthorized overtime
4. Not tracking breaks properly
5. Keeping inaccurate or incomplete records
6. Not compensating interns or volunteers
7. Failing to stay up-to-date with regulations

Determining the Applicability of the Fair Labor Standards Act

When determining whether the FLSA provides protection to a particular worker, three questions can determine whether a particular worker is afforded no protection, some protection, or complete protection under the FLSA. To determine FLSA applicability, determine coverage for

1. **Employers** – All employers have some federal law protecting their workforce. Only particular

enterprises are not covered by the FLSA. Any employer that is primarily engaged in education or the care of the sick, is a public agency, or is an organization with an annual revenue of $500,000 or more is likely covered by the FLSA.[16]

2. **Workers** – The FLSA protects employees but does not provide the same protections for independent contractors. Whether a worker should be classified as an employee or an independent contractor is one of the first assessments an employer must make when hiring.

3. **Employees** – Once a worker is properly identified as an employee, the employer must then determine whether the employee is exempt from the FLSA's overtime provisions or nonexempt.

Employer Exclusions

The vast majority of jobs are covered by the FLSA. However, there are two instances in which an entire occupation may be excluded from the FLSA:

1. A job may be excluded from FLSA protections because the act explicitly calls for its exclusion. Employees of certain establishments and in certain occupations may be excluded from FLSA

rules, such as employees of seasonal or recreational establishments.

2. A job may be completely excluded from FLSA minimum wage and overtime pay protections because it is regulated by another labor statute. This usually applies to unique industries. For example, railroad workers have the Federal Labor Act, a majority of truck drivers are covered by the Motor Carriers Act, and agricultural workers have their own federal statute protections and are not covered by the FLSA.

Employee Misclassification Hazards

> *In 2018, an Oregon judge required an owner of three courier companies to pay $3,087,100 to his drivers for misclassifying them as independent contractors, in addition to paying $112,900 in penalties.*[17]

Laws to Know

A worker is afforded FLSA minimum wage and overtime protections if the worker is identified as an employee as defined by the FLSA. Independent contractors are not considered employees entitled to these FLSA protections. The FLSA defines an *employee* as "any individual employed by an employer," and defines *employ* as including "to suffer or permit to work." These definitions were

> Misclassifying workers as independent contractors when they should actually be identified as employees is an all too common mistake.

intentionally drafted to include as broad a range of workers as possible.[18]

Misclassifying workers as independent contractors when they should actually be identified as employees is an all too common mistake by employers. There are harsh consequences for this mistake, such as employers paying high penalties. Such fees may include paying back wages, back taxes, insurance premiums, penalties for each misclassified worker, and even legal fees for the employers' own counsel and the employees'. This is a topic that should not be overlooked. The stiff penalties associated with a violation make it worth reexamining periodically at least annually.

Common misclassification scenarios consist of

1. **Commonly Violated Industries** – Particular industries more commonly misclassify workers as independent contractors as a result of traditional employment relationship dynamics and control retained by employers in those industries. A couple of examples of industries in which this violation happens more frequently than others include the construction industry's hiring independent contractors, or salon industry's hiring stylists as independent contractors but retaining control over their schedule, products, clients, etc.

2. **Franchise Arrangements** – Situations in which the overseeing franchisor retains a high level of control over the independent franchisee could result in the employees of the latter being recognized as employees of the franchisor.

3. **Volunteers** – Employees cannot volunteer their time doing work that they would otherwise be doing as an employee.

4. **Trainees or Apprentices** – Depending on the circumstances, unpaid trainees or apprentices may also be recognized as employees under the FLSA.

5. **At-Home Workers** – Workers who operate from their own homes are often quick to be characterized as independent contractors, however, the FLSA may cover such workers as employees.[19]

How Employee-Contractor Status Is Determined

As a best practice, employers should default to treating every worker as an employee, unless confident the definition of independent contractor has been met. There are multiple tests for distinguishing employees from independent contractors depending on which law is being applied. Different enforcement agencies may apply different tests. For example, a worker who is identified as an independent contractor under the FLSA, may be an

Employers should default to treating every worker as if they are an employee.

employee under a state law, or vice versa. While the FLSA grants federal protection, there are a number of different state agencies that apply their own tests, such as the state departments of labor and industries (handling state insurance), state employment offices (handling unemployment matters), or state supreme courts.

FLSA's Employee-Contractor Test

Laws to Know

The first test all employers should consider when determining whether their workers should be classified as independent contractors versus employees is the FLSA test. Under the FLSA, if workers are economically dependent upon the employer, they will be considered employees, versus independent contractors who are in business for themselves. This is referred to as the **economic reality test**. When assessing economic reality, the courts look to a number of various factors, although no single factor is determinative. Some of the common factors considered include

1. the extent to which the work performed is an integral part of the employer's business,
2. the nature and degree of control by the employer,
3. the amount of investments by workers in facilities and equipment,

4. the workers' skill and the initiative required to be successful,

5. the permanency of the relationship between workers and employer, and

6. whether the workers' managerial skills affect their opportunities for profit and loss.[20]

States' Differing Tests

Most states model their various tests for identifying employees from independent contractors on the economic reality tests used by the FLSA, or at least use analogous factors. This, however, does create some ambiguity for employers attempting to properly characterize their workers, because certain factors may be given substantial weight in one incident, but may not be as persuasive in another. As such, some states, although not many, have adopted stricter tests that substantially deviate from the traditional economic reality test. It is worth either reviewing the applicable laws or consulting an employment law expert.

For example, in California, the State Supreme Court has recently drastically altered the test to distinguish an independent contractor from an employee. Employment experts are still figuring out how to navigate this new legal terrain.[21] For more about laws distinguishing employees and contractors, see "Additional Information" at the end of the chapter (page 65).

TIPS TO AVOID MISCLASSIFYING INDEPENDENT CONTRACTORS

It becomes evident that multiple standards must be considered to ensure that workers are correctly classified. Employers should take additional steps beyond those required by the FLSA to ensure that workers are classified correctly. Employers should review all applicable laws and attempt to adhere to the most constrictive standards to help ensure compliance.

Even when applying the most constrictive standards for identifying workers, many employers become confused and unsure whether they have properly classified their workers, and reasonably so. The multitude of tests—each considering several different factors, while possibly placing more persuasive weight on certain factors than others—would create uncertainty for almost any employer.

For additional protection, employers should require a contract with each independent contractor they do business with. This contract should at least explicitly state that workers

1. are free from control by the employer;
2. provide their own equipment and materials;

3. have been hired for a specific project or a limited period, and the relationship is not ongoing;
4. are tasked with projects outside the typical operations of the employer;
5. have their own business IDs or tax IDs;
6. are responsible for their own taxes; and
7. are responsible for their own costs and expenses.

It is not enough to merely have a contract outlining these aspects of employment; it must be consistently applied and practiced. While a contract helps establish credibility for the employer, in the end the court assesses the actions and whether these restrictions were adhered to.

Minimum Wage and Overtime Exemptions

Correctly classifying employees can be difficult even for labor and employment experts. Zenefits, a human resource management company, recently had to pay $3.4 million in unpaid overtime to 743 of its employees for misclassifying them as exempt from minimum wage and overtime.[22]

Although employers must determine whether their workers should be classified as employees or independent contractors, the analysis doesn't stop there. Once an employer has properly identified a worker as an employee under the FLSA, the employer must determine whether the employee is considered exempt or nonexempt under the FLSA.

Child Labor Provision Exemption – "Youth younger than 16 years of age working in nonagricultural employment in a business solely owned by their parents or by persons standing in place of their parents, may work any time of day and for any number of hours. However, parents are prohibited from employing their child in manufacturing or mining or in any of the occupations declared hazardous by the Secretary of Labor." (U.S. Department of Labor).

Exempt employees may be excluded from FLSA overtime pay protections, minimum wage protections, or both, or its child labor protections. Here I will mainly focus on the common exemptions from both the FLSA's minimum wage and overtime requirements.

Although the majority of employees covered by the FLSA are nonexempt, employees may be exempt from FLSA overtime rules for one of two reasons. First, a small amount of jobs are exempt based on the jobs themselves. For example, outside sales employees are exempt, yet inside sales employees typically are nonexempt.[23] Second, the more common reason a covered employee may be exempt is because the position satisfies a three-part test based on job duties and rates of pay. Each of the criteria must be satisfied.

Although there are exceptions, for workers to be exempt employees, the FLSA requires that they must

(a) be paid on a salary basis,

(b) be paid a salary minimum of at least $23,660 annually or $455 per week (increased to $684 per week or $2,964 monthly beginning 2020), and

(c) perform specific "primary duties" within one of the enumerated exemptions.[24]

I. Salary Basis Test

To be exempt under the FLSA, generally the employee must be compensated on a salary basis. Salary, as recognized by the FLSA, is a fixed, predetermined, regular amount of compensation, paid on a (bi)weekly, monthly, or another predetermined basis. Employers may pay their employees more than the guaranteed salary amounts, e.g., bonuses, and still maintain their salary basis status because it does not result in reductions to their base pay.[25]

There are particular occupations in which being compensated on a salary basis is not required to be exempt under the FLSA, such as attorneys, doctors, and schoolteachers.

An alternative to the salary test that employers, especially those working in sales, should be aware of is compensation on a **fee basis**. Fee basis compensation is relevant for employees whose primary duties fit the executive, administrative, or computer exemption category (discussed later). If they are paid a single, set amount for work completed on a single, unique project, then they are paid on a fee basis. For this to apply, the amount paid to the employee must equate to or be greater than what minimum wage would have compensated that employee for the time worked.[26]

II. Minimum Salary Test

Laws to Know

Next, for employees to be exempt, their salaries must meet or exceed the salary minimum. Currently, the minimum salary provision requires that an exempt employee earn at least $23,660 annually, or $455 per week. With very few exceptions, employees who are paid less than $23,600 per year ($455 per week) cannot be considered nonexempt.[27]

However, as of January 2020, the salary requirement has been increased to a rate of not less than $684 per week or $2,964 monthly. The employee must meet or exceed the salary threshold every pay period. There are, however, circumstances in which an employer can make deductions from an employee's salary.[28]

Salary Deductions

Under the FLSA there are permissible and impermissible deductions to exempt employees' salaries. Permissible deductions are allowed without forfeiting employees' exempt status. Employers should be mindful of how they define "salary" and under what circumstances they allow for salary deductions. Deductions to employees' base salaries

> Employers should be mindful how they define "salary" and under what circumstances they allow for salary deductions.

that reduce their pay below the salary basis minimum or other impermissible salary deductions may negate any exempt status employees have under the FLSA.

(a) *Impermissible Deductions* – Generally, these include any reduction in salary based on poor performance, emergency closings, quantity of work, quality of work, partial absences, and other similar reasons. Such unauthorized deductions by the employer, if excessive enough, could negate any impression that the employee is compensated at a level satisfying the minimum salary test.

Employers should only allow for permissible salary deductions to include unpaid FMLA leave, extended unpaid absences, and unpaid suspensions.

(b) *Permissible Deductions* – Salary deductions generally are not permissible under the FLSA. However, as a best practice, employers should only allow for permissible salary deductions to include reductions to time of unpaid leave under the Family and Medical Leave Act (FMLA), unpaid absences from work extending beyond a week, and unpaid suspensions of a full day or more. Additionally, employers should make it clear when onboarding a salaried employee what the authorized salary deductions are.

(c) *Quasi-Deductions* – Instead of making salary deductions for extended absences, employers should require that salaried employees charge their extended absences to their leave accruals. This would not be considered a deduction in pay under the FLSA, because the dollar amount on the employee's paycheck would remain unchanged.[29]

Safe Harbor Policy for Improper Deductions

When employers make improper deductions or violate overtime provisions for a salaried employee, they risk losing exempt status for that employee under the FSLA, and not only for that employee, but possibly for all employees similarly situated or within the same classification. Recognizing that employers may unintentionally violate this provision and want to remedy the situation upon discovery without highlighting the mistake and inviting a lawsuit, the FLSA has allowed for a safe harbor policy to protect employers for unintentional violations. Under this protection, an employer will not forfeit the salary basis criteria of the exemption for the employee(s), if the employer

1. has a clearly communicated policy that explicitly prohibits improper deductions and includes a process that allows employees to notify management of potential errors,
2. reimburses employees for any improper deductions that are discovered, and

3. makes a good faith commitment to comply in the future.

As with nearly all safe harbor policies, the best way to ensure that something is clearly communicated is to place it in the employee handbook where all employees can find it. This will be discussed further in the following chapter.

III. Primary Duties Test

After determining that an employee meets the salary requirements to be considered exempt from the FLSA overtime protections, an employer must then assess whether the employee's primary duties meet the criteria for a specific exemption. The FLSA has carved out specific jobs for exempt employees; they typically are limited to employees with high-level duties and responsibilities. Whether a position qualifies for an exemption depends on that position's specific duties.

Laws to Know

Primary duties, as applicable to the FLSA, are described as "the principal, main, major, or most important duty that the employee performs. Determination of an employee's primary duty must be based on all the facts in a particular case, with a major emphasis on the character of the employee's job as a whole."[30] The definition goes on to state that "employees who spend more than 50 percent of their time performing a specific duty will generally satisfy the primary duty requirement."[31]

As such, the title of the position provides very little persuasive value in the analysis. Salesman are still a salesman even if they are called administrative assistants, and chief financial officers are still CFOs even if they are called janitors and happen to pick up their own trash every once in a while. The duties test focuses specifically on the actual job tasks regularly performed and how they fit into the employer's overall operations. Even disparity of pay between exempt and nonexempt employees may be a factor considered.[32]

Common Exemptions

The majority of employees identified as exempt from FLSA overtime provisions fall into one of five common exemption categories based on their primary duties. Exemptions are strictly construed under a narrow interpretation of the exemption and the position's primary duties. When an exemption is challenged as having been inappropriately applied, the burden is on the employer to prove otherwise. As such, employers must be mindful to assess the actual duties of the position and conditions of the exemption applied. The position's actual duties and responsibilities should be consistent with the position's job description before declaring that it fits into a particular exemption just because of the title.

Some of the most commonly used exemptions are the executive, administrative, professional, computer, and outside sales exemptions. A brief summary of the general primary duties necessary for each exemption is provided below to help employers make initial assessments whether any are applicable to their employees. If employers feel that any are applicable to their employees, a deeper dive into the actual duties of the exemption is recommended (to learn more about FLSA exemptions, see "Additional Information" at the end of the chapter on page 65).

Exemptions are strictly construed under a narrow interpretation of the exemption and the position's primary duties. When an exemption is challenged as having been inappropriately applied, the burden is on the employer to prove otherwise. As such, employers must be mindful to assess the actual duties of the position and conditions of the exemption applied.

1. *The Executive Exemption* is directly related to the management of the employer's business.
2. *The Administrative Exemption* is directly related to the general business operations of the employer or the employer's clients.
3. *The Professional Exemption* requires specialized academic training for entry into a professional field. Under this broad category, there are essentially two industries:

    (a) The *Learned Professional Exemption* covers work requiring advanced knowledge customarily acquired by a prolonged course of specialized intellectual instruction in a field of science or learning.

(b) The *Creative Professional Exemption* covers work in a recognized field of artistic or creative endeavor. Typically, workers who fall into this category include actors, various artists, musicians, composers, journalists, and possibly teachers.

4. *The Computer Exemption* covers those in the computer field. Worth noting is that workers who are commonly misplaced in this category generally include engineers, drafters, and others skilled in computer software design.

5. *The Outside Sales Exemption* covers those making sales away from their employer's place of business.[33]

TIPS FOR DETERMINING EMPLOYEE EXEMPTION STATUS

Even after determining that an employee should be classified as exempt, there are numerous factors and conditions that must be consistently met. To help ensure that an employee is properly classified for exemption status, ensure the following:

1. The employee is compensated on a salary basis, usually recognized by a predetermined

basis. Otherwise, the employee must be compensated on a fee basis.

2. The employee's compensation must meet, or even better, exceed the salary minimum: at least $23,660 annually or $455 per week (increased to $684 weekly or $2,964 monthly beginning in 2020).
3. Any salary deductions are for permissible purposes, such as FML.
4. There is a clearly communicated safe harbor policy in place for improper deductions.
5. The primary duties for employees who are considered exempt meet the criteria for their specified exemptions.

Compensating Employees for All Hours Worked

In 2017, TGI Friday's settled a nationwide lawsuit for 19.1 million in response to allegations of wage theft, specifically, for failing to pay 28,000 workers proper minimum wage, overtime pay, and misappropriated tips. As well as, inappropriate time-recording practices that resulted in unpaid "off-the-clock" work, such as requiring workers to

> *arrive a hour early to complete "side-work," clock in after they received their first table, and punch out prior to completing their side-work.*[34]

A frequent mistake by employers of all sizes is not compensating employees for all hours worked, especially in incidents in which employees accrue unauthorized overtime. Under the FLSA, all nonexempt employees must be paid for all hours worked, regardless of whether they were unauthorized or off-the-clock.

> A frequent mistake by employers of all sizes is not compensating employees for all hours worked, especially in incidents in which employees accrue unauthorized overtime.

The FLSA considers work that is off-the-clock, meaning work that is unpaid or not counted toward overtime, as illegal. It does not matter if an employee comes in early to do prep work or a dedicated worker stays late to finish a project, all work "suffered or permitted" must be compensated for and counted toward overtime.

Overtime and Off-the-Clock Work

The FLSA requires nonexempt employees to be paid overtime for working beyond forty hours a week. Federal law defines employment to include work that is "permitted or suffered" from the employee's activity. An employer requesting employees to work would clearly be permitting work. An employer may have to compensate an employee for work that was not explicitly permitted, but the work is "suffered" nonetheless. Suffered work is work that the employee engages in that is not solicited but is allowed, such as clocking out and staying late to complete tasks or to assist colleagues.[35]

If an employee has worked the hours, pay them for the hours, even if the work was unauthorized.

As a best practice, if an employee has worked the hours, pay the employee for the hours, absent extenuating circumstances. The employer still has the right to discipline the employee for not getting approval to work off-the-clock. Keep in mind, however, that the discipline should not appear as retaliation for voicing a workplace violation (i.e., nonpayment) but for not following workplace expectations (i.e., to get approval before working unauthorized hours).

Common violations regarding off-the-clock work and overtime include unpaid time for:

(a) *preparation*, including setup, warming up, or putting on safety equipment;

(b) *post-shift work*, such as clean up, close-outs, and other uncompleted daily tasks, and also includes travel time to locations at which employees must conclude their days;

(c) *administrative work*, such as reviewing documents, meetings with management, or completing trainings that should be paid;

(d) *revising work*, which often includes the time employees spend correcting mistakes or redoing and improving prior work; and

(e) *waiting for work when none is immediately available*, which usually includes the time employees are required or allowed to wait around for projects, and is a common violation with hair salons or barbershops.

Meal Breaks

The FLSA does not require employers to provide meal or rest breaks to their employees. It does, however, place restrictions on employers who choose to offer meal breaks, such as:

(a) *Compensated Breaks* – Rest breaks provided of twenty minutes or less must be paid by the employer.

(b) *Uncompensated Breaks* – The employer is not required to compensate employees for meal breaks lasting thirty minutes or more.

(c) *Determining Overtime* – When calculating total hours worked for overtime, breaks of twenty minutes or less must be considered in the sum as time worked.

(d) *Unpaid Means Not Working* – If employees are not compensated for meal breaks, they must be entirely relieved of all work duties. A common violation occurs when employees work, even minimally, while on unpaid meal breaks. Simply having responsibilities, even passive duties not requiring any proactive behavior, is enough to create liability for the employer (e.g., an employee having to supervise a group of individuals, who may even happen to be in the same area as the employee who is taking a break).[36]

State Restrictions Regarding Breaks

Despite FLSA or other federal laws requiring meal and rest breaks for employees, every state has varying requirements on employers regarding breaks. For more about applicable state laws on meal and rest breaks, see "Additional Information" at the end of the chapter (page 65).

Donning and Doffing

Under the FLSA, employers are required to compensate their employees for "all time during which an employee is necessarily required to be on the employer's premises, on duty, or at a prescribed workplace."[37] As such, there are certain circumstances in which employers are legally required to pay their employees for time spent putting on and taking off certain work clothes and protective equipment. This is referred to as "donning and doffing."

> Employers should be mindful of this if they require their employees to wear uniforms, especially if employees must change and put on work equipment at the worksite.

When, exactly, donning and doffing is compensable under the FLSA is an area of law that is very unsettled, so each circumstance should be looked at on a case-by-case basis. When taking a more conservative approach, employers should compensate employees for time spent donning and doffing if the employees' actions are (1) necessary to the principal work performed and (2) where the primary benefit to the employer.

The employer should be compensating the employee for any activity recognized as integral or indispensable to the position's regular duties.

Employers should be mindful of this if they require their employees to wear uniforms, especially if employees must change and put on work equipment at the worksite. As a best practice, if an activity is recognized as an integral part or indispensable to the position's regular duties, the employer should compensate the employee for that time. Putting on safety equipment would generally be recognized as an integral part of or indispensable to a position, especially if safety concerns are involved. The time that the employee spends putting on or removing these work clothes or protective gear while at the worksite should be recorded as paid time.[38]

Setting Expectations

Additionally, supervisors and managers need to be thoroughly trained on break expectations and emphasize these expectations with employees. Oftentimes, despite good policy, employees still feel pressured to clock out for their breaks but continue working due to workplace pressures or other reasons. Despite employees' good intentions to be productive workers and the employer's good intention of offering breaks, it only creates liability to allow employees to take unpaid breaks in which they still work.

Despite employees' good intentions to be productive workers and the employer's good intention of offering breaks, it only creates liability to allow employees to take unpaid breaks in which they still work.

Time Tracking Software

Employers not tracking breaks or lunches properly is an underlying cause for many workplace violations and is a common violation in and of itself. One tool employers can use to combat this issue is a time and attendance software program that can assist tracking this information, which is required by law in some states.

TIPS FOR TIME RECORDING AND OVERTIME POLICIES

Nearly every employer needs to establish workplace policies making clear the expectations for recording hours, getting authorization to work unscheduled shifts, meal breaks, overtime, etc. These policies need to clearly lay out expectations for unauthorized or off-the-clock work and should be placed somewhere easy to find in the employee handbook. Such policies can include language like the following:

- Employees must record all their time worked correctly.
- Employees must review and then sign their time records to confirm their accuracy and that there was no unauthorized or off-the-clock work performed that was not recorded.
- Employees may not falsify or instruct another to falsify time records or misrepresent their hours worked.
- Employees must promptly notify HR or management of any time record errors.
- Any and all alterations to time records must be done by HR or management only; no exceptions.
- Any mishandling, alteration, or falsification of time records should be reported to HR or management immediately.
- Employees are only allowed to work preauthorized hours, including overtime; no exceptions.

- Employees are not allowed to begin working early, late, or throughout their meal breaks without prior authorization, and any such time worked must be recorded; no exceptions.

- Employees who violate any of these policies may be subject to discipline, up to and including termination.[39]

Additional tips on drafting a strong safe harbor policy for deductions and time recording are available in the following chapter, "Employee Handbook," under "Time Recording Policies" (page 81).

Additional Information

- Defining Common Exemptions – **The Fair Labor Standards Act, 29 CFR Part 541**, https://www.law.cornell.edu/cfr/text/29/part-541.
- List of Exemptions in the FLSA – **U.S. Department of Labor, Employment Laws Assistance for Workers and Small Businesses**, Fair Labor Standards Act Advisor, https://webapps.dol.gov/elaws/whd/flsa/screen75.asp.
- Information Regarding States' Distinguishing Employees and Independent Contractors – **DOL, Wage, and Hour Division**, State Labor Offices, https://www.dol.gov/whd/contacts/state_of.htm.

- Applicable State Laws on Meal Breaks – **DOL, Wage, and Hour Division**, "Minimum Length of Meal Period Required under State Law," https://www.dol.gov/whd/state/meal.htm.
- Applicable State Laws on Rest Breaks – **DOL, Wage, and Hour Division**, "Minimum Paid Rest Period Requirements under State Law," https://www.dol.gov/whd/state/rest.htm.

3

Why You Need an Employee Handbook

Employee handbooks are extremely vital pieces of evidence in any employment lawsuit. With the median cost of attorney fees for an employment case that goes to trial being $88,000,[40] *it is so surprising that according to a 2017 survey only 26 percent of small businesses with less than ten employees had employee handbooks.*[41]

The employee handbook is a tool that can make management's job easier by setting clear expectations, providing guidance and direction to employees, and helping to mitigate liability exposure for the employer. Although there are no federal or state laws that require employers to have handbooks, employers are required by law to notify their workers of various employee rights. The employee handbook serves as a great tool to notify employees of these rights.

Objections and Benefits

There are a few common reasons why employers do not have handbooks. These need to be overcome. Let's take a closer look:

1. *Complexity/Don't Know How* – When employers who understand the value of a handbook are asked why they still don't have one, the response typically is that they don't know how to create one or even where to begin. The goal of this chapter is to provide employers with the basic knowledge of essential policies and disclaimers that all handbooks need to include, along with examples of model language as a starting point for nearly every employee handbook.

2. *Time/Costs* – Often employers complain that it will either take them too long to create a handbook or that it will cost too much to have a professional draft one for them. It is understandable to not want to invest time or money into a product that may not appear to directly benefit the company's bottom line. However, when compared to the cost of potential litigation or even an unproductive workforce, taking proactive steps can save the employer hundreds of thousands, even the company itself in the long term. As mentioned previously, companies

have gone bankrupt from litigation costs and heavy judgments.

3. *Tie Employers' Hands/Limit Flexibility* – Occasionally an employer will say that they want to handle matters on a case-by-case basis, and a handbook will only tie their hands or limit what they can do. There is some truth that a handbook's policies will establish practices and procedures for handling certain matters, but this is a good thing for employers. As discussed later, the sections and policies that need to be in nearly every handbook are matters that should be handled in a consistent manner to mitigate liability (e.g., personnel decisions handled inconsistently can create liability exposure for a claim of discrimination for disparate treatment) and improve efficiency (e.g., management doesn't have to explain to every employee the process for issuing sick leave or overtime each time it is requested).

4. *Unintentionally Create a Contract/Liability* – The fear of unintentionally creating a contract on behalf of the employer with an employee is the most common reason why employers usually reach out to professionals to draft their handbooks. While it is possible to unintentionally create an implied contract by using certain verbiage in the handbook (e.g., for guaranteed

employment or benefits), this chapter will provide key disclaimers and tips on policy verbiage to address this concern.

Creating an employee handbook may seem like a daunting task, but having one can be an invaluable asset for an employer and its employees. **Here are seven reasons why every employer needs an employee handbook:**

1. *Serves as an Introduction to the Company Culture* – The introduction section of the handbook is a great opportunity to let employees know what the company is about. This section should talk about the company culture, such as whether there is an emphasis on teamwork, results, employee engagement, responsibility and accountability, and learning opportunities. In addition to describing how the employee will fit in, the introduction can have information on the company and its history, such as how it was started, what sets it apart, and what its vision is. The introduction of the handbook sets the standard for the employee-employer relationship and provides a guidepost for the remaining policies.

2. *Notifies Employees of Workplace Expectations* – The handbook is a guide for employees to navigate their employment relationship. It needs to provide clear policies and procedures for addressing

matters related to their employment, especially outside of their specific position duties. For example, it lays out the process for taking a sick day or requesting overtime. It also clearly explains safety standards and practices, such as not showing up intoxicated. The handbook states what the expectations are for interacting with coworkers and customers in the workplace. If the employer so chooses, a standard of conduct should be explicitly detailed.

3. *Provides a Guide for Working with Management and Leadership* – A handbook should be a guide advising employees of procedures for certain matters. It should clearly explain to whom employees should report matters, what they can expect in response from company leadership, and what the process entails following employee reporting. There are processes outside of the daily duties of a position that could discourage an employee from coming forth or cause confusion if not thoroughly explained. For example, employees need to know to whom they should report safety concerns, discrimination, or harassment, or request FML leave or Americans with Disabilities Act (ADA) accommodations.

Employees need to know to whom they should report safety concerns, discrimination, or harassment, or request FML leave or ADA accommodations.

4. *A Guide for Management and Maintaining Consistency* – As much as the handbook is a guide for employees, it can also be a guide for managers to ensure consistent application when making personnel decisions. For the handbook to have any value it is vital that its policies are consistently applied. Known and understood policies and standards that are consistently applied not only help prevent liability exposure but also help foster trust with management. A clear understanding of policy and procedure helps combat the fear of being targeted or disparate treatment. For example, if expectations regarding cell phone use while at work are not known and some employees are disciplined for it at various levels of discipline, while others are not disciplined at all, management not only loses trust with its employees, but this type of action can also lead to claims of discrimination.

For the handbook to have any value it is vital that its policies are consistently applied.

5. *Attracting Talent by Showcasing Employment Entitlements and Benefit Packages* – An employee handbook can be used as a recruitment tool. It is a resource that employers can direct applicants to that lays out the company's benefit packages and entitlements, such as longevity pay, vacation, retirement information, etc. A handbook

can also be a place to look for incentives available for purposes of retention. For example, the handbook may include common retention practices, such as the various opportunities the company creates for upward mobility, whether the company prioritizes hiring from within, opportunities to transfer to other work locations, paid trainings offered, etc.

6. *Satisfies Legal Obligations* – While employers are not required to have a handbook for their employees, they are required by law to notify employees of certain rights and ensure that certain processes are followed. The handbook serves as an excellent platform to communicate company policies on such topics – for example, whether the company requires that meal breaks be taken by the fifth hour – as a practice to ensure compliance (state laws may vary). Other examples may include time recording policies, state disability leaves, federal FMLA leave, and other government mandates. The handbook is where these expectations should be communicated.

Employers are required by law to notify employees of certain rights and ensure that certain processes are followed.

7. *Helps the Organization Defend Against Employee Lawsuits* – In addition to using the handbook to notify employees of certain employer obligations

and rights, the handbook can serve as a vital tool in defending the company against potential lawsuits and employee claims that will inevitably happen for many employers. A thorough and compliant handbook that is consistently adhered to can demonstrate that the employer exercised "reasonable care" toward its employees. Having an employee-signed acknowledgement page will demonstrate that the employee read, understood, and agreed to the company policies and procedures outlined in the handbook and will help create an affirmative defense the employer can use in litigation. It may also satisfy notice requirements (e.g., where to report sexual harassment) which may limit liability, enhance the employer's jury perception in the event of a lawsuit, and possibly curb lawsuits before they even begin. Examples of other policies in a handbook that help create a defense to certain employee claims may include essential disclaimers (i.e., At-Will, EEO employer), anti-discrimination and anti-retaliation policies, reporting policies, investigation procedures, etc.

Essential Policies

> *"In many employment lawsuits, your handbook will be a key piece of evidence that can either protect your company or provide ammunition for the employee (or former employee) who is suing you."*[42]

An employer may understand how it could benefit from using an employee handbook, but common questions still arise, such as what topics should be covered in an employee handbook, how much information to include, and how specific or vague it needs to be. There are a wide range of topics employers can include in the employee handbook, but employers need to balance their goal of being clear and specific with not including so much unnecessary information that the handbook essentially loses its effectiveness. Employers cannot expect their employees to familiarize themselves with a handbook the size of a textbook. This section will walk through some of the common and recommended sections all employers need to consider including in a handbook.

An employer's goal when creating an employee handbook should be to provide general guidance to employees regarding the employment relationship, include key disclaimers and legally required notices, assist the employer in mitigating liability and risks, clearly communicate the employer's values and priorities, establish workplace expectations, and assist with workforce management without restricting management's discretion. A handbook promoting these goals needs to include, at a minimum, policies and procedures addressing

- discrimination and harassment,
- workplace violence,
- social media,
- wage and hour reporting,
- FLSA (at-will or exempt),
- meal and rest breaks,
- leave,
- misconduct or a standard of conduct,
- employee discipline,
- reporting procedures, and
- disclaimers.

Anti-Harassment/Discrimination

If an employer chooses to have an employee handbook, it is recommended that it include anti-discrimination and anti-harassment policies. Anti-discrimination and anti-harassment policies are exactly what they sound like, an explicit statement that the employer does not tolerate any form of discrimination or harassment within its company, whether it be initiated by an employee, supervisor, manager, customer, etc. (For additional information on workplace discrimination and harassment, see the "Discrimination, Harassment, and Retaliation" section in the following "Employee Misconduct" chapter on page 104).

It is a good practice to explicitly title the policies the "Anti-discrimination Policy" and "Anti-Harassment Policy" to help demonstrate that the employer has clearly communicated and put employees on notice. Additionally, it's good practice to include in this policy that (1) discipline may be issued for any acts held to be discriminatory or harassing in nature; (2) the organization has a commitment to nondiscrimination and anti-harassment; (3) encouragement of reporting such acts and directions how employees may lodge such complaints; (4) a statement that the company will promptly take action and initiate investigations; and (5) an assurance that there will be no retaliation for reporting.

> If you do include examples, you must state that they are just examples and "the list is not exhaustive."

Additionally, it is important to give some examples as to what discrimination and harassment may look like in the workplace. However, if you do include examples, you *must* state that they are just examples and "the list is not exhaustive." Common examples of what may be considered workplace discrimination and harassment include

(a) jokes or demeaning statements based on race, religion, sexual orientation, gender, or national origin;

(b) unwelcome touching;

(c) jokes of a sexual nature; and

(d) disrespectful conduct (vague language used to include conduct not captured otherwise in this policy).

Workplace Violence Policy

It is a good practice for every employee handbook to include an explicit workplace anti-violence policy. Similar to an anti-harassment policy, a workplace anti-violence policy generally is exactly what it sounds like: a policy that explicitly states that the employer will not tolerate any violence of any type in the workplace.

It is important to have one because it puts all employees on notice of what the expectations are. It is an explicit policy that can be used as authority if the need ever arises to discipline a worker for unacceptable behavior. Additionally, a workplace anti-violence policy mitigates liability if the employer should ever face a lawsuit or other legal action for an incident involving violence in the workplace.

This policy needs to be clearly defined and easy to find. As a best practice, employers need to label the policy the "Workplace Anti-violence Policy" or something similar.

At the very least, the policy needs to include (1) an explicit statement that violence is not allowed in the workplace; (2) an expectation that all workers will comply with this policy, including management and various workers (e.g., contactors, employees), in addition to customers and members of the public on company property; (3) an encouragement to report all violations immediately and procedures for reporting, listing at least two different sources; (4) an assurance that the employer will investigate and promptly take action; and (5) an assurance that there will be no retaliation for reporting.

Employers need to label the policy the "Anti-Workplace Violence Policy" or something similar.

Additionally, as mentioned with other sections, it is generally best practice to include examples of what constitutes workplace violence. However, if you do include examples, you need to state that they are just examples and "the list is not exhaustive." Common examples that may be considered workplace violence include

(a) unwelcome touching,

(b) intimidating or menacing postures or actions, and

(c) threats of violence or harm.

Social Media and Company Device Use Policy

It is recommended that employers include a social media policy in their employee handbook. A social media policy is one that lays out expectations relating to employee's use of social media, as well as expectations relating to use of company devices. This is a topic on which the law has been growing and developing recently.

A social media policy must strike a balance between employers' needs and employees' rights to privacy. It cannot be overly restrictive or too intrusive. Some state laws have already identified certain actions as being too intrusive to the point of violating employees' rights to privacy. (See "Off-Duty Behavior and Social Media" on page 142 for additional information on attempting to access or investigate an employee's social media account). These intrusive and potentially illegal acts include

1. employers requiring that employees share their social media login information, and
2. employers requiring access to view employees' social media pages, even if private.

Because this is a hot topic that will be growing and developing for the foreseeable future, employers should take a conservative approach when drafting policies on this topic and include only minimal restrictions (to learn more about the protections in place restricting employer access to employees' social media, see the "Additional Information" section at the end of the chapter on page 99).

This policy needs to include the explicit statement, "Social media can implicate company policies and standards of conduct." Meaning that if employees conduct themselves on social media in such a way that can be construed as violating *any* of the company policies, they can be disciplined for it just the same as if they did it in the workplace.

For employers who allow employees to use company equipment and electronics, such as a company phone, laptop, or workplace server, include a policy statement that there is no expectation of privacy for such use of company equipment. Meaning that the employer has a right to search and have access to company equipment and all information contained within them. The law weighs almost entirely in favor of employers over employees' rights to privacy when it concerns company equipment.

Most wage and hour disputes stem from misunderstandings or lack of clarity on expectations relating to reporting off-the-clock work or time-recording practices.

Time Recording Policies

Wage and hour disputes are a common source for many lawsuits that employers face. Most wage and hour disputes stem from misunderstandings or lack of clarity on expectations relating to reporting off-the-clock work or time-recording practices. As such, employers need to establish very clear policies on what the company's expectations are regarding recording hours, getting authorization to work shifts, overtime, meal breaks, etc. These policies need to be placed somewhere that is easily identifiable in the employee handbook. Such policies can include language similar to the following:

(a) Employees must record all their time worked correctly.

(b) Employees must review and then sign their time records to confirm their accuracy and that there was no unauthorized or off-the-clock work performed that is not recorded.

(c) Employees may not falsify or instruct another to falsify time records or misrepresent their hours worked.

(d) Employees must promptly notify HR or management of any time record errors.

(e) Any and all alterations to time records must be done by HR or management only; no exceptions.

(f) Any mishandling, alteration, or falsification of time records should be reported to HR or management immediately.

(g) Employees are only allowed to work preauthorized hours, including overtime; no exceptions.

(h) Employees are not allowed to begin working early, late, or throughout their meal breaks without prior authorization, and any such time worked must be recorded.

(i) Employees who violate any of these policies may be subject to discipline, up to and including termination.

Employers need to make it a priority that all employees be reminded of these policies on a periodic basis, especially if it is discovered that employees are not consistently following these policies by working off-the-clock or not reporting their hours.

Exempt Employees – Salary Violation Policy

Most employers have FLSA exempt and nonexempt employees. Nonexempt employees are paid on an hourly basis, in which time recording is a high priority, given that it dictates employees' compensation. Exempt employees, typically supervisors or managers, are compensated on a salary basis (see the "Minimum Wage and Overtime Exemptions" section in the "Wage and Hour Laws You Need to Know" chapter on page 47). Although exempt employees are usually not compensated on an hourly basis, they should be held to the same standard as nonexempt

> Employers need to consider implementing a policy to protect against exempt employee salary violations, such as improper deductions.

employees for recording their time, especially because there might be deductions affecting their salary. As such, employers need to consider implementing a policy to protect against exempt employee salary violations, such as improper deductions. This policy needs to include the following key provisions:

(a) The company shall follow all applicable laws and pay all employees appropriately for all time worked.

(b) Salaried employees shall be paid a fixed, predetermined, regular amount of compensation, on a (bi) weekly, monthly, or another predetermined basis.

(c) For partial work-day absences, the company shall allow deductions from employees' sick or vacation leave banks (whichever applicable), and such deductions shall never be taken from employees' salaries, even if leave banks are exhausted.

(d) Full-day absences for personal reasons shall first be deducted from employees' vacation leave banks, however, if exhausted, may be deducted from employees' salaries.

(e) Employees are to review their records for errors and improper deductions.

(f) Only deductions permissible by law shall be allowed, such as (identify which types of absences will be allowed, whether there are deductions for medical and dental premiums, 401Ks, etc.).

(g) Potential errors and improper deductions should be reported to HR or management immediately for prompt investigation.

(h) Employees shall be reimbursed for any discovered errors or improper deductions.

(i) Employees will not be retaliated against for reporting errors or participating in investigations.

A policy including these provisions will help employers avoid liability exposure by explicitly stating what the employers' practices are, demonstrating that employees are on notice of such expectations and procedures, and communicating a remedial process that employees can initiate in the event errors are made.

Meal and Rest Breaks

Contrary to general belief, not all workers are guaranteed meal or rest breaks by federal law, although many states have their own requirements for breaks (paid or unpaid). It is the employer's responsibility to make sure that workers comply with these requirements. A meal and rest break policy needs to state the employer's expectations of when and how employees take their required breaks. Many states' laws differ from each other, especially as to when these breaks must be taken by the employee (for more information on applicable laws regulating employee meal breaks, see "Additional Information" at the end of the chapter on page 99).

Require that employees take their meal breaks prior to the times required by law.

If an employee does not take a meal break consistent with state laws, the employer will be liable, regardless of the circumstances as to why the employee did not take the break. This could result in the employer being subjected to heavy fines by the state. As such, the employer's expectations need to be clearly laid out in the handbook. It should state that employees are to take their meal breaks consistent with applicable law. A best practice is to take a conservative approach with the policy by requiring that employees take their meal breaks prior to the times required by law. Additionally, be sure to state in the policy that not adhering to this policy can result in discipline, up to and including termination.[43]

Leave

Federal state and local laws grant different forms of leave to employees. Some laws, depending on the location and jurisdiction, may require that notice be given to employees of their rights to certain forms of leave. As such, it is always good practice to include a section in an employee handbook, or in a policy provided elsewhere, that explicitly notifies employees of their different rights to leave.

> When drafting policies regarding employees' rights to leave . . . be mindful not to unintentionally create a contract that grants employees a vested right to the leave, unlimited accruals, or an expectation for payout of leave on termination of employment.

Common variations of leave include family and medical leave (FMLA), military leave, paid parental leave, domestic violence leave, maternity leave, disability leave, employer provided vacation, sick leave (paid or unpaid), and other forms of extended time off, such as sabbatical.

When drafting policies regarding employees' rights to leave, how it's administered, and how to request various forms of leave, be mindful not to unintentionally create a contract that grants employees a vested right to the leave, unlimited accruals, or an expectation for payout of leave on termination of employment. At the least, policies regarding leave should clearly communicate

(a) what forms of leave employees have a legal right to,

(b) which forms of leave are discretionary to the employer,

(c) how employees accrue additional leave,

(d) the process for requesting leave,

(e) the process for reintegration following return from extended leave, and

(f) assurances that the company will not retaliate

against employees who have requested or taken leave.

Standard of Conduct

A standard of conduct outlines the employer's expectations regarding employees' behavior toward their coworkers, customers, and the organization overall. The policy may include behavior addressed in other company policies or may be used as a catch-all policy for behavior not fitting in a workplace that does not necessarily constitute violence, harassment, or behavior otherwise addressed elsewhere in the handbook. Additionally, a standard of conduct can be used to address expectations of employees in unique circumstances, such as using company equipment, reimbursement expectations, etc.

This policy can be as specific or as general as the employer wants it to be. Depending on the nature of the business, it may be prudent to list all the unacceptable behavior a new employee would likely not be aware of unless notified. Examples of behavior to be addressed in a standard of conduct may include

(a) potential conflicts of interests,

(b) accepting gifts,

(c) culture competency expectations,

(d) respectful business communications or other unacceptable behavior,

(e) company equipment use,

(f) company reimbursement expectations, and

(g) a drug-free workplace.

Issuing (Progressive) Discipline

Discipline should be based on a pattern of alleged behavior, harm caused, and malicious intent.

When faced with a lawsuit, employers must defend any disciplinary action they issue an employee, whether it be a suspension, demotion, termination, etc. One of the best ways to do this is to have explicit policies in place prohibiting certain behaviors and laying out the procedures used to determine an appropriate level of discipline (see Chapter Five, "Discipline, Discharge, and Documentation," on page 149). When determining what level of discipline to issue, it is a best practice to consider discipline based on (a) a pattern of the alleged behavior, (b) harm caused, and (c) whether there was any malicious intent. For violations that are not egregious, it is recommended that employers use progressive discipline prior to issuing severe consequences.

Progressive discipline is the process of increasing the penalties for repeated violations. If employees have a contract stating that they can only be fired for just cause, then going through the various levels of progressive discipline is recommended for non-egregious acts. Just cause ensures that employees are afforded sufficient due process for any disciplinary actions that they may face. Although most employees are at will—meaning terminable for any reason or no reason at all (as long as it is not discriminatory)—employees with just-cause protection are not at will. If they are not at will and have just-cause protection, in order to issue severe discipline for non-egregious acts employers usually must demonstrate that they have issued lower-level discipline prior to issuing far more severe discipline, such as termination.

The various levels of discipline can take many forms, such as a coaching and counseling, verbal warnings, written reprimands, short-term suspension, long-term suspension, demotion, and termination.

If no employees within an organization have just-cause protection, listing the various forms of discipline may not be necessary, but still may be good to include. However, be sure not to use language that requires that the employer use progressive discipline, especially if they don't have to. Including language that gives the employer discretion to issue various levels of discipline is recommended.

> Be sure to give multiple options for reporting that include different individuals at the managerial level who do not report to one another.

Internal Complaint Procedure

It is important for employers to lay out clear and easy-to-navigate reporting procedures for all concerns. Employees need to understand whom to go to with issues or concerns, and what the procedure is for reporting violations or any improper actions. Be sure to give multiple options for reporting that include different individuals at the managerial level who do not report to one another. If an employee feels intimidated by a supervisor or high-level executive, there needs to be another place or person that employee can go to and not be fearful that the alleged violator has power to circumvent the reporting and investigatory process.

One example of a complaint procedure is for the employees to contact HR (or a similarly situated high-level executive), high-level manager (e.g., director, VP, etc.), or a supervisor.

It is just as important to train management on what to do when employees come to them with concerns. Inconsistent responses to reports of harassment, discrimination, or other workplace issues can be invitations to lawsuits.

TIPS FOR DRAFTING ESSENTIAL POLICIES FOR EMPLOYEE HANDBOOKS

There are a few general policies that all handbooks need to include to explicitly reserve certain rights to employers. These policies are also important to grant employers the right to revise these policies in the future and to grant flexibility to employers in administering such policies.

Additionally, there are a few tips on words to avoid and phrases to include in order to help protect employers from lawsuits.

All employee handbooks need to

1. Require that all employees sign a page at the end of the handbook acknowledging that the employee is in receipt of the handbook and its policies and that it does not form a contract.

2. Be sure *not* to include any language of absolutes, like "must," "shall," or "will," but instead allow for some flexibility and discretion for the employer by using verbiage such as "may," "shall consider," "can lead to," or "could result in." (Use the word-find computer tool to search for absolute-style verbiage.)

3. When giving lists of examples, explicitly state that they are only some examples and the "list is not exhaustive" or that it is "including, but not limited to" the examples stated.

4. *Never* hide information. Do not make any essential policies or key disclaimers difficult to find by burying them in the middle of other information, making them too small, not including appropriate titles for the information,

or placing them in locations in the handbook that would be difficult to notice. If it is not easy to find, a court can hold that the employer did not actually put the employee on notice of that information.

5. The handbook should be consistently enforced to ensure its effectiveness. The handbook is only effective to the degree to which the employer consistently and objectively adheres to its own policies. It can create liability for the employer if certain processes and procedures are not consistently enforced.

Key Disclaimers to Include

A court held that an employee handbook with clear promissory language and no disclaimer that it "could be changed at the employer's discretion or that it did not form a contract" resulted in the employee handbook creating an implied contract, requiring an employer to compensate its truck driver for 30 percent of the gross income received by both companies for loads he had driven, $15 an hour for detention and layover pay, and 70 percent coverage of his health insurance, spanning his eight-year employment.[44]

There are a handful of disclaimers that nearly all employers need to include in their employee handbooks. Two that speak to conditions of workers' employment are the Equal Employment Opportunity ("EEO") disclaimer and an At-Will Employment disclaimer, if applicable. An additional two disclaimers speak to conditions of the handbook itself, including a disclaimer that the handbook is only a set of guidelines and in no way forms a contract with the employee, as well as a disclaimer reserving the employers right to modify the handbook at any time. Each of these disclaimers can be thought of as a legal safety net that provides some of the bare minimum employment rhetoric needed to put employees on notice. Demonstrating that employees have been put on notice helps establish some of the basic elements needed to prevent or defend against certain lawsuits.

No Implied Contract Disclaimer

Every handbook needs an explicit statement notifying employees that the handbook in no way is intended to create a contract, implied or otherwise. This policy can be as direct as stating, "The policies, procedures, and standard practices described in this manual are not conditions of employment. This manual does not create an express or implied contract between [Employer] and any of its employees."

Employer Right to Modify Disclaimer

In addition to including a statement to help protect against unintentionally creating an implied contract for employment, employers should include an explicit statement that reserves their right to modify, change, and deviate if necessary from the policies and procedures within the handbook. Although it is recommended not to deviate from established practices and policies, a statement reserving that right to the employer needs to be included for situations requiring exceptions. Additionally, it is impossible to foresee every possible workplace scenario and what the appropriate response should be until it actually happens. As such, a disclaimer stating, "The employer reserves the right to make changes to this handbook and its policies at any time," helps employers maintain flexibility and their rights to deviate from the handbook.

Place this disclaimer in one of the first three pages of the handbook or immediately following the table of contents.

Equal Employment Opportunity (EEO) Disclaimer

All employee handbooks need to contain an equal employment opportunity policy that needs to be prominently placed in a very easy-to-find location. As a best practice, it is recommended that this disclaimer be placed in one of the first three pages of the handbook or immediately following the table of contents. This policy is the first legal protection from a discrimination lawsuit and can be an essential tool in defending employers from substantial liability. Given the importance of this policy, instead of explaining what it should contain, an example of one that could fit most organizations is provided below. **If you make any changes to it, which is not recommended, only add to it but do not remove any of the statements, because each one has a purpose and provides its own protection.**

> [Company Name] provides equal employment opportunities (EEO) to all employees and applicants for employment without regard to race, color, religion, sex, national origin, age, disability, or genetics. In addition to federal law requirements, [Company Name] complies with applicable state and local laws governing nondiscrimination in employment in every location in which the company has facilities. This policy applies to all terms and conditions of employment, including recruiting, hiring, placement, promotion, termination, layoff, recall, transfer, leaves of absence, compensation, and training.
>
> [Company Name] expressly prohibits any form of workplace harassment based on race, color, religion, gender, sexual orientation, gender identity or expression, national origin, age, genetic information, disability, or veteran status.

> Improper interference with the ability of [Company Name]'s employees to perform their job duties may result in discipline up to and including discharge.

At-Will Employment Disclaimer

As discussed earlier, an at-will employee is one who has no right to employment and can be terminated for any reason or no reason at all (as long as it is not discriminatory). An at-will policy is a disclaimer that puts the employee on notice of this relationship. For employers with at-will employees, unless there is a specific reason not to, the employee handbook needs to include an at-will policy. Similar to the EEO disclaimer, this notice needs to be clear, concise, and easily identifiable by prominently placing it in a very easy-to-find location within the handbook. An example of one may state the following:

> Your employment with [Employer Name] is at will. This means that your employment is for an indefinite period of time and it is subject to termination by you or [Employer Name], with or without cause, with or without notice, and at any time.

TIPS FOR DISCLAIMERS

1. Include a statement in the handbook that clearly characterizes the handbook as just a set of guidelines that it in no way forms a contract with the employee.
2. Include a disclaimer stating that "The employer reserves the right to make changes to this handbook and its policies at any time."
3. Have an "EEO Disclaimer" and an "At-Will Employment Disclaimer" in your handbook.
4. Disclaimers need to be prominently placed in a very easy-to-find location, preferably within one of the first three pages of the handbook or immediately following the table of contents.
5. Each disclaimer should have an explicit title, identifying what the policy is.
6. It is recommended that if you use the example model disclaimers provided, you only add to them but do not remove any of the statements, because each one has a purpose and provides its own protection.

Additional Information

- State Protections Restricting Employer Access to Employees' Social Media – **National Conference of State Legislatures**, "State Social Media Privacy Laws," http://www.ncsl.org/research/telecommunications-and-information-technology/state-laws-prohibiting-access-to-social-media-usernames-and-passwords.aspx.
- Applicable State Laws on Meal Breaks – **DOL, Wage, and Hour Division**, "Minimum Length of Meal Period Required Under State Law," https://www.dol.gov/whd/state/meal.htm.

Employee Misconduct

4

Workplace misconduct can cost employers millions if not addressed appropriately. This is demonstrated well in a 2014 lawsuit filed by Osama Saleh, a twenty-eight-year-old, Yemeni-born American citizen and practicing Muslim. Saleh made several complaints to his manager about a coworker's repeated bullying behavior, such as calling him names like "Bin Laden," "dirty Arab," and "terrorist."

The manager took no disciplinary action against the coworker and failed to address the misconduct or attempt to prevent it from continuing. Predictably so, the misconduct continued and escalated, until it culminated in the coworker punching Saleh and knocking him unconscious. Despite the manager's attempts to minimize the employee's experience by saying that it was "no big deal" and that they were just "teasing each other," the jury disagreed and ordered the store to pay $4.7 million in compensatory and punitive damages.[45]

Why You Need to Be Concerned About Workplace Misconduct

In 2018, the EEOC received 76,418 complaints for various types of discrimination.[46]

Employee misconduct is generally defined as a substantial or intentional disregard of the employer's interests. Usually, the employee's intent to disregard such interests is a crucial component when determining whether an employee's conduct constitutes misconduct. Regardless of how each employer defines misconduct, it is important for employers to make clear to employees that it will not be tolerated, what types of acts may constitute misconduct, and that employers will respond consistently to similar acts of misconduct for each employee.

An employer should view all of its employees as agents of the business. This means that all employees have the potential to create liability on behalf of the employer. Additionally, the employer is responsible for maintaining a safe working environment for these employees. As such, injuries to employees resulting from unsafe working conditions or from misconduct, including harassment or discrimination, of which the employer knew or should have been aware, usually creates liability on behalf of the employer.

Despite what might feel like a legal death trap, an employer can protect itself by maintaining a safe working environment through good policies and procedures, and by implementing best practices when responding to complaints or notices of misconduct and safety concerns.

Bullying, Violence, and Safety Concerns

Workplace bullying, violence, and safety hazards must be taken very seriously by employers because they can be liable for them, especially if not responded to correctly. Bullying has been defined as "abusive conduct that is (1) threatening, humiliating, intimidating, or (2) work interference – sabotage – that prevents work from getting done, or (3) verbal abuse."[47] In many contexts employee bullying, as well as workplace violence, constitutes harassment. Additionally, various states have recently implemented workplace anti-bullying laws that prohibit workplace bullying in government workplaces, with many other states also considering doing the same.[48] (For more information on other states' workplace anti-bullying initiatives, see "Additional Information" at the end of the chapter on page 147). As such, every employer should protect itself by having at a minimum a policy prohibiting bullying and workplace violence, and a clear structure for reporting complaints.

Laws to Know

The employer has an obligation to take all complaints seriously, especially safety concerns, whether it's a harmful substance in the air or a report of a dangerous individual on the worksite. Once an employer is aware of a safety concern or should have been aware, they are liable for not taking prompt remedial action to address it.[49]

Laws to Know

Some examples of safety concerns that employers must promptly respond to include

(a) needing protective wear,

(b) a suspicious or disgruntled customer or employee,

(c) an employee operating machinery under the influence,

(d) a firearm on the worksite (good idea to have a policy prohibiting firearms), and

(e) altercations between employees or between employees and supervisors.

Discrimination, Harassment, and Retaliation

Most employers know that they should prevent discrimination and harassment from happening in the workplace. However, most employers aren't sure what that entails. The consequences for allowing discrimination or harassment to occur will likely result in lawsuits, with very high litigation costs, embarrassment for employers and the individuals involved, stress, time associated with handling such matters, and an invitation for others to act the same, as well as an invitation for more lawsuits.

Unchecked misconduct also has an impact on the workforce, affecting morale, turnover, productivity, and the ability to attract or keep talent, among others. As such, properly addressing discrimination and harassment matters should be a priority for every employer. While addressing these matters may seem daunting, especially to an employer with no HR background, there are proactive steps that can be taken to mitigate discriminatory matters from arising in the first place and to help protect the employer if a lawsuit were to occur.

The first step employers should take when addressing discrimination and harassment in the workplace is to familiarize themselves or a company representative on the various applicable anti-discrimination laws. Although various laws use different tests to assess for discrimination and harassment, generally discrimination is recognized as prejudicial treatment in the workplace that affects employees' employment—their money, such as, hiring, firing, promotions, salaries, or layoffs—that is based on an individual's age, gender, sexual orientation, race, religion, national origin, disabilities, or another protected class. Whereas, harassment is recognized as unwelcome conduct that is discriminatory or sexual in nature. This unwelcome conduct must be severe, pervasive (i.e., continuous), or a condition of employment.[50]

Laws to Know

> *Employers should be familiar with all the protected classes identified in the applicable laws.*

Anti-discrimination Laws

Nearly all employers are subject to federal, state, and local laws regarding discrimination. As such, it is best practice to be familiar with all the protected classes identified in each applicable set of laws. There are federal protections against various forms of discrimination under a compilation of federal acts passed over the last half century, such as:

Race/Color, Gender, National Origin, and Religion – The Civil Rights Act of 1964 (Title VII), the most comprehensive of the federal anti-discrimination protections, protects against discrimination based on these protected classes.

Age – The Age Discrimination in Employment Act (ADEA) makes it a violation to discriminate against current or prospective employees over the age of forty. Employees under forty are not protected from age discrimination by federal law, but they may be covered by state laws.

Citizenship – The Immigration Reform and Control Act of 1986 makes it a violation to discriminate against workers or applicants based on their citizenship or immigration status.

Disability – According to the Americans with Disability Act and the Rehabilitation Act, employers cannot discriminate against current or prospective employees based on any physical or mental disability or previous medical condition, such as cancer. The employer also must make reasonable accommodations in the workplace for these employees.

Equal Pay – The Equal Pay Act requires employers to pay employees equal pay for equal jobs, despite the person's gender, age, race, religion, national origin, or disability.

Pregnancy – The Pregnancy Discrimination Act forbids employers from discriminating against women in the workplace due to pregnancy, and the employer must provide reasonable accommodations when necessary.

Genetic Information – The Genetic Information Nondiscrimination Act of 2008 makes it a violation for an employer to discriminate against workers based on their genetic information.

In addition to federal protections, there are also state and local laws, each usually more restrictive and providing more protections against discrimination than federal laws. These laws may create anti-discrimination protections for breastfeeding women, marital status, familial status (including status as a caregiver to a family member), political beliefs and activities, sexual orientation, gender identity, military status, veteran status, or criminal record. Although federal laws may not protect unpaid interns and volunteers against discrimination and harassment in some circumstances because they are not recognized as employees, some state and local laws may (for more information regarding the various state anti-discrimination laws, see the "Additional Information" section at the end of the chapter on page 147).

Employers must be mindful that anti-discrimination laws also protects individuals from retaliation for filing discrimination charges, testifying, or participating in any way in investigations, proceedings, or lawsuits under these laws; or opposing employment practices that they reasonably believe discriminate against individuals, in violation of these laws.

Have a staff member designated to maintain a firm understanding of the applicable anti-discrimination laws.

As a best practice, it is recommended to designate a staff member to maintain a firm understanding of the applicable anti-discrimination laws and be responsible for handling such issues when they arise. This individual should be the same person identified in any anti-discrimination and harassment policies as the person to report complaints to.[51]

Preventing, Responding, and Investigating Misconduct

> *"Nearly half of HR professionals say their organization had at some point experienced a workplace violence incident at some level—up from 36% in 2012. Of those who reported having experienced workplace violence, more than half said their*

organization had experienced an incident in the last year."[52]

After developing a basic understanding of the applicable anti-discrimination laws, employers need to be proactive. Employers must take preventive measures to protect their employees from harassment and others' misconduct by implementing efficient procedures to address such behavior when it does occur. Not only does taking these steps help foster safer and more positive working environments, which generally translates into a productive workforce, but it protects employers from what otherwise could be substantial and expensive litigation. In *Burlington Industries, Inc. v. Ellerth*, the court held that employers are not liable for workplace discrimination or harassment when "(1) the employer exercised reasonable care to prevent and correct any harassing behavior and (2) that the plaintiff unreasonably failed to take advantage of the preventive or corrective opportunities that the employer provided."[53] Subsequent courts agreed, as in *Vance v. Ball State University*.[54] An essential first step to demonstrate "reasonable care to prevent and correct any harassing behavior" is having a sound anti-discrimination policy, according to the EEOC.[55]

Laws to Know

Anti-Discrimination and Anti-Bullying Policy

A sound anti-discrimination policy at the very least should inform employees that

1. Harassment or discrimination is strictly prohibited and may result in discipline, up to and including termination.
2. Employees are encouraged to report misconduct immediately, and the company will not tolerate any retaliation for reporting misconduct or participating in an investigation of the same.
3. Procedures are in place regarding to whom they should report any concerns, which provide for more than one option.
4. Concerns of discrimination or harassment will be investigated immediately.

It is vital for employers to make sure that all employees, including managers, are notified of the policy and know that the employer takes such matters very seriously. Requiring that employees sign and date the policy as proof that they received and reviewed it is recommended; proof of receipt could be vital in a lawsuit. Courts have held that "dissemination of 'an effective anti-harassment policy provides proof' that an employer exercised reasonable care to prevent and correct . . . harassment."[56] Additionally, the EEOC recommends that employers require all employees, especially managers, to be regularly trained on this protocol.[57]

Reporting Structure

Any sound discrimination policy should make clear to employees to whom they can report allegations. *The policy should contain multiple options for reporting potential violations.* The EEOC recommends that "if possible, designate at least one person outside an employee's chain of command who can receive harassment complaints. Consider permitting employees to report harassment to any manager." If the employer's reporting procedure allows for an employee to go to multiple managers or executives, they all must be trained on how to respond properly, consistently and in a timely manner to all allegations.[58]

> . . . if possible, designate at least one person outside an employee's chain of command who can receive harassment complaints. Consider permitting employees to report harassment to any manager.

How to Respond to Allegations of Misconduct

The employer does not have discretion to pick and choose which allegations to take seriously. All allegations of harassment should be taken seriously and promptly investigated. They should be handled in a fair and consistent manner. Handling allegations in a consistent manner includes what remedial action is taken, such as the issuing of disciplinary actions against an employee found to have engaged in the inappropriate behavior, if necessary.[59]

> Assume each complaint could potentially become a lawsuit in which the entire investigative file, including notes and correspondence, could end up as subject to discovery in determining whether the employer's response to the allegation was adequate.

Having a thorough and fair investigation for each allegation is important. Assume each complaint could potentially become a lawsuit in which the entire investigative file, including notes and correspondence, could end up as subject to discovery in determining whether the employer's response to the allegation was adequate.

(a) *Focus on Internal Investigation* – The investigation should focus on whether a workplace policy of misconduct was violated, and not focus on whether the alleged act meets some legal standard of discrimination or harassment. This is one of the reasons it is important to have an explicit misconduct policy or standard of conduct.

As a best practice, avoid using legal terms that may be difficult to defend against if the matter were to escalate into a lawsuit. For example, it is difficult to defend against a discrimination lawsuit if the employer has an investigation file saying it found that there was indeed "discrimination," yet is accused of failing to take corrective action. In investigations, notes, and documents, it is best to use "misconduct" or "violation of policy," not "harassment," "retaliation," or "discrimination."

Avoid using legal terms that may be difficult to defend against.

(b) *Be Consistent in Investigation Procedures* – Employers must be sure to be consistent in following their own procedures in conducting investigations for all allegations raised. Employers should remain neutral, fair, bias-free, and thorough in responding to all allegations.

i. *Prompt Action.* One factor that will be assessed when determining whether the employer responded to misconduct appropriately is how much time it took for the employer to follow up and address the allegation. Employers should be consistent in taking immediate action in response to allegations of misconduct. Generally, an investigation should be initiated immediately after receiving a complaint or becoming aware of a serious issue. Failing to respond in a consistent and timely manner can create liability. Additionally, resolving issues early can greatly reduce the chances of an EEOC charge and can assist the employer in defending against a lawsuit.

ii. *All Allegations.* An employer should not be selective regarding which complaints it takes seriously. To be consistent and fair, the employer's complaint procedure needs to be an effective remedial tool for all. As such, it cannot filter out complaints without giving each due diligence. Also, by responding to allegations in a consistent manner, the employer protects itself from being liable for disparate treatment by treating employees differently. As stated earlier, if the employer's reporting procedure allows for an employee to go to multiple managers or executives, they must all be trained on how to respond properly, consistently, and in a timely manner to all allegations.

(c) *Use an Experienced Investigator* – An employer's response to an allegation of harassment or any other violation should be fair and effective. To demonstrate a fair and thorough investigation, it should be conducted by an investigator who is trained and experienced in handling the specific type of investigation needed. Additionally, the investigator should be someone disconnected from the day-to-day operations of the business. This person should be recognized by employees as an objective official, without a vested interest in the outcome of the investigation—typically an HR director or outside investigator.

How to Investigate Misconduct – The Essentials

The EEOC recommends that all investigations of misconduct contain at least the following actions by the investigator, regardless whether it is a claim of harassment, discrimination, workplace violence, or threat of violence:[60]

(a) *Interviewing the Complainant* – Generally, every investigation should be initiated by first interviewing the complainant who raised the allegation. The complainant is not always the victim in every situation. There may be incidents that are witnessed or known by a coworker or a colleague who then brings the alleged act to the attention of management. In following up with the complainant, the investigator should ask questions that ascertain the facts and details, such as starting off the interview with the "who," "what," "when," and "where" of the allegation.

If the investigation was not initiated through a general written-complaint procedure (that should be established), it is important for the investigator to get a written statement from the complainant. This can be done at the conclusion of the initial interview with the investigator, if it has not already been completed.

(b) *Obtaining a Written Statement from the Person Raising the Concern* – A written statement detailing the allegation is vital for many reasons. A written statement serves as the documentation and written record of the specific allegations the investigator is to investigate. This helps prevent a situation in which the complainant, at the conclusion of the investigation, claims additional allegations were failed to be investigated. A written record also prevents the complainant from exaggerating or fabricating further allegations. It is not uncommon in events of unfounded allegations for the complainant to bring up, at the conclusion of an investigation, additional acts that were not initially mentioned.

It is not uncommon in events of unfounded allegations for the complainant to bring up, at the conclusion of an investigation, additional acts that were not initially mentioned.

Additionally, having complainants give written statements in their own writing is more descriptive and gives better insight to the allegations, based on their word choices. Furthermore, it makes it more difficult for complainants to allege that the investigator minimized or mischaracterized the severity of the allegation if it is the complainant's own descriptive language.

(c) *Interviewing Subject to the Complaints* – When investigating the subject of the complaints, it is important to relay that the investigation will be done thoroughly and fairly, that the investigator is a neutral party to the investigation, and that the individual is not presumed to be guilty. It is also important to state that untruthfulness may result in severe consequences, up to and including termination.

Ask about each specific instance of misconduct alleged. Be sure not to group allegations or neglect to inquire into specific allegations just because there may be numerous instances alleged.

Remind the interviewee that the purpose of the interview is to determine the validity of the allegations and not to have a conversation to negotiate the severity of potential discipline that may result.

If the employee admits to the allegations, acknowledge that such actions are inappropriate and in violation of company policies, and that the employer will get back to the employee at a later time with whatever action it will take in response.

If the allegations are denied, ask if there's any evidence that can be supplied that corroborates the employee's recollection of events, such as emails, documents, or witnesses.

Remind interviewees at the end of the interviews that if they think of any additional information or have anything to share that they forgot to mention or said they would supply as corroboration, they can always follow up with such information after the interview. It is a best practice to let them know how much longer the investigation will likely go and when they need to provide additional information to the investigator, if they plan to.

(d) *Interviewing Witnesses* – Often interviewees, especially the accused, will recommend a large number of additional employees, or sometimes individuals not even with the employer, whom they believe should be interviewed as "witnesses." While it is a best practice to ask interviewees if they recommend that anyone else be interviewed, it is the investigator's job to filter through these recommendations and prioritize interviewing witnesses who can corroborate incidents mentioned and the complainants' allegations.

When interviewing witnesses, it should be emphasized that the purpose of the interview is to determine whether employees violated company policies, which the company takes seriously.

Investigators should ask witnesses if anyone tried to influence their participation in the interview, and whether they were pressured not to partake or to say certain things.

For the same reasons as requesting a written statement from the complainant, it is recommended to require written statements from the witnesses, as well. This can be done by asking witnesses to write their statement, or having the investigator summarize the interviews and having the witnesses review and sign the investigator's summaries or notes.

Equal Employment Opportunity Commission Guidelines

Even though different investigators may have varying styles in how they carry out discrimination or harassment investigations, the Equal Employment Opportunity Commission (EEOC) provides clear and helpful guidelines regarding the specific questions that should be asked in the interviews. These guidelines provide a good framework for the various interviews and should be followed whenever possible. They address the necessary elements that demonstrate a fair and thorough investigation by an employer.[61]

(a) *Recommended Questions for the Complainant* – When interviewing the complainant, the individual who brought forth the allegation, the EEOC recommends asking the following questions, if applicable:

- Who, what, when, where, and how: *Who* committed the alleged inappropriate conduct? *What* exactly occurred or was said? *When* did it occur and is it still ongoing? *Where* did it occur? *How often* did it occur? *How* did it affect you?
- How did you react? What response did you make when the incident(s) occurred or afterwards?

- How did the inappropriate conduct affect you? Has your job been affected in any way?
- Are there any persons who have relevant information? Was anyone present when the alleged incident occurred? Did you tell anyone about it? Did anyone see you immediately after episodes of alleged inappropriate conduct?
- Did the person who harassed you harass anyone else? Do you know whether anyone complained about inappropriate conduct by that person?
- Are there any notes, physical evidence, or other documentation regarding the incident(s)?
- How would you like to see the situation resolved?
- Do you know of any other relevant information?

(b) *Recommended Questions for the Alleged Harasser* – When interviewing the person who allegedly engaged in the misconduct, the EEOC recommends asking the following questions:

- What is your response to the allegations?

- If the harasser claims that the allegations are false, ask why the complainant might lie.
- Are there any persons who have relevant information?
- Are there any notes, physical evidence, or other documentation regarding the incident(s)?
- Do you know of any other relevant information?

(c) *Recommended Questions for the Witnesses* – When questioning witnesses, the EEOC recommends asking:

- What did you see or hear? When did this occur? Describe the alleged harasser's behavior toward the complainant and toward others in the workplace.
- What did the complainant tell you? When did s/he tell you this?
- Do you know of any other relevant information?
- Are there other persons who have relevant information?[62]

Determining Witness Credibility

Conducting a fair and thorough investigation requires more than simply asking the right questions. It also requires the investigator to properly weigh and interpret the responses, i.e., to determine the credibility of the parties interviewed. Fortunately, the EEOC also provides factors employers can assess to help determine credibility.[63] These questions can be used by employers to document their decision-making process and bolster the validity of their findings regarding the credibility of the complainant, alleged harasser, and witnesses. The EEOC provides the following guidance to assess credibility:

- **Inherent Plausibility**: *Is the testimony believable on its face? Does it make sense?*
- **Demeanor**: *Did the person seem to be telling the truth or lying?*
- **Motive to Falsify**: *Did the person have a reason to lie?*
- **Corroboration**: *Is there* witness testimony *(such as testimony by eye-witnesses, people who saw the person soon after the alleged incidents, or people who discussed the incidents with him or her at around the time that they occurred) or* physical evidence *(such as written documentation) that corroborates the party's testimony?*

- **Past Record**: *Did the alleged harasser have a history of similar behavior in the past?*[264]

TIPS TO HELP ADDRESS WORKPLACE MISCONDUCT

1. Once employers are aware of safety concerns, or should have been aware, they are liable if they do not take prompt remedial action to address them.
2. Every employer should have an explicit policy prohibiting bullying, workplace violence, and discrimination, and a clear structure for reporting complaints to more than one individual.
3. Be familiar with various applicable anti-discrimination laws.
4. Designate a staff member to maintain a firm understanding of the applicable anti-discrimination laws and to serve as the main person to report complaints to.
5. To help avoid liability, employers should use reasonable care to prevent and address misconduct in the workplace, such as consistently looking into all allegations immediately after

becoming aware of them, as well as using an experienced investigator.

6. Use the helpful guidelines provided by the EEOC to assist with conducting a proper investigation.

Developing Areas of Employment Law

> *For employers, trying to stay compliant with the constant changes and additions to employment-related law can feel like a dog trying to catch its tail—In 2018 alone, at least twenty-seven states and key municipalities modified or enacted new workplace protections.*[65]

Although most areas of employment law are longstanding and well understood, there are other areas of law that employers must keep a watchful eye on. These areas are tricky because they are new areas of law and issues to deal with, so the law is still growing and developing. For example, employees' use of social media is a new subject that the law hasn't fully adapted to yet and is quickly growing. This section will touch on some of these developing areas of employment law and provide some best practices and conservative approaches aimed at limiting liability.

Alcohol, Marijuana, and Drug Use

Generally, in the private sector, employers may test employees for drugs but are not required to. Those employers who are required to test are likely in industries that are heavily regulated or have federal contracts. These specific industries and contracts may require employers to take reasonable steps to prohibit employees from working under the influence and to maintain drug-free workplaces, such as those employers covered by the Drug-Free Workplace Act. While federal law is mostly silent about drug testing, many states and local governments do regulate employer drug testing.

Various Applicable Laws Regulating Drug Testing

(a) *The Drug Free Workplace Act* – In order to receive a federal contract or grant of $100,000 or more, this Act requires that federal contractors or grantees agree to provide drug-free workplaces. This act applies a zero-tolerance standard for drug use, including marijuana. However, it does not provide how an employer must maintain a drug-free workplace. What the act does require is that the employer "make an ongoing, good-faith effort to maintain a drug-free workforce," have a published drug-use policy and drug-free awareness program, with penalties or rewards for participating. Although the employer must also report any employee workplace criminal drug convictions, there is no requirement to test employees for drugs.[66]

(b) *Americans with Disabilities Act (ADA)* – Despite there being no comprehensive federal law regulating drug testing in the private sector, the ADA places some regulations on medical examinations in general. The ADA prohibits medical examinations unless the employer can demonstrate that they are "job-related and consistent with business necessity." Additionally, the ADA makes it illegal to discriminate based on a disability. Federally recognized illegal drugs are not protected under the ADA, so no rationale is needed to test for them. However, alcohol is protected. Under the ADA, an alcoholic may be determined to be an "individual with a disability." While marijuana is legal in many states in some form, it is still illegal federally, even for medicinal purposes, and therefore, is not protected under the ADA. For employers in states that provide protection for marijuana use, medicinal or otherwise, it is recommended to treat marijuana drug testing the same as alcohol testing for safe measure. As such, the employer should have a strong business rationale to test for alcohol or marijuana, but no rationale under the ADA is needed to test for other drugs.[67]

(c) *State/Local Governments* – Nearly all states allow employers to conduct some form of drug testing of applicants or employees. However, most states or local governments require the employer to follow specific parameters, such as providing adequate notice of testing to the applicant or employee, or following specific testing procedures to protect against discrimination or inaccurate samples. For an example of how one state chose to handle this issue, see the box below. Employers should review applicable laws on this subject prior to initiating employee drug testing. More information on potentially applicable laws regulating employee drug testing can be found under "Additional Information" at the end of the chapter (page 147).[68]

Washington State Addressing Drug Use in the Workplace:

Drug testing applicants under Washington law (RCW 49.127.1; WAC 356-46-125, §356-05-128) is "authorized with advance written notice to applicant and after conditional offer of employment has been made." For currently employed workers in the private sector, drug testing is authorized with "60 days' notice to employees, in cases of workplace accidents, as part of an employee assistance program, on reasonable suspicion of substance abuse, or at random. Employers' written substance abuse policy must be posted and distributed to employees. State agencies can test on reasonable suspicion—stated in writing—for safety-sensitive positions pursuant to a written testing policy."

As it relates to marijuana, Washington passed I-502 which made marijuana legal for medical and recreational purposes. However, employers still have a right to regulate the use or impacts of marijuana and alcohol in the workplace. I-502 does not specifically address the topic of drug-testing, however, it has been generally understood that employers may continue to drug-test in accordance of their legally adopted policies.

At the time of directing an employee to submit to a drug test, include the business rationale for requiring the examination.

The Importance of Legally Verified Rationales for Drug Tests

It is a best practice to include the business rationale for requiring the examination at the time of directing the employee to submit to the drug test. Many states require employers to verify a cause for testing currently employed workers for substances. It helps build credibility of the employer's intent to have the business rationale already articulated in writing and notify the employees prior to testing.

One of the strongest and most frequently cited business rationales to justify drug testing for employees is a safety concern. Particularly for employees with specific safety concerns embedded into their job duties, such as operating heavy machinery, employers should take steps to ensure the safety of their employee, as well as the customers or public. Positions with safety concerns embedded in their job duties should have these concerns explicitly stated in the job description. Otherwise, it may be harder to justify the drug testing as a safety requirement. Other common reasons employers may choose to drug test their employees include reducing injury risk, improving workforce productivity, mitigating insurance costs, and reducing turnover.

When Testing Is Allowed

After employers have determined that they can justify drug testing and decided that they want to, then they must determine when to carry out the testing. Just because employers can test their employees, doesn't mean that employers can go about it whenever and however they want to. Certain states place restrictions and parameters on when drug testing is allowed or prohibit drug testing in certain circumstances altogether. This section will give some guidance on the various times an employer may subject an applicant or employee to drug testing. The common types of employee drug testing include pre-hire, random testing, reasonable suspicion, and post-incident.

State that drug testing will be a part of the application process in the job application and at every step of the interview process.

(a) *Pre-Hire/Applicant Testing* – Many states allow for applicant testing. Common restrictions for drug testing applicants include

i. putting the applicant on notice that such drug testing will be a part of the application process for new employees (best practice is to state this in the job posting and application, at every step of the interview process, and to provide the applicant with the Drug Testing Policy at the initial interview and ask them to review it if they are called back for a follow up or an offer);

ii. making an offer of employment contingent upon passing a drug test;

iii. ensuring consistency in requiring all offers for the position or similar positions be contingent upon submitting to drug tests; and

iv. following applicable requirements when testing, such as using designated state-administered testing agencies, testing only for specific substances, or using specific collection methods.

(b) *Random Testing* – Random testing and blanket drug tests of all employees are very effective because they are unpredictable. However, many states and local governments have either outlawed these types of drug tests or placed restrictions on them because they are not focused on the individual and cannot be justified by a legitimate business rationale. As such, it is a best practice not to conduct random drug testing of individuals, especially blanket workforce drug testing. Random alcohol testing is also an issue under the Americans with Disabilities Act and is not recommended either.

If random drug testing is performed, it is best to use a computer-generated random selection. This provides an additional defense if an employee were selected multiple times and claimed discrimination.

(c) *Reasonable Suspicion Testing* – When an employer has a reasonable suspicion that an employee may be under the influence during work hours, in violation of a company policy, the employer may direct the employee to submit to a drug test, also known as "for cause testing." The reasonable suspicion must be based on objective facts and logical inferences. While "reasonable suspicion" may seem to vary depending on who is making the determination, there may be applicable state laws defining what "testing for 'reasonable suspicion'" is. Lisa Guerin, an employment law specialist and author, has compiled some examples of actions supporting reasonable suspicion that an employee may be violating workplace intoxication policies:

> The reasonable suspicion must be based on objective facts and logical inferences.

- "direct observation of drug use or its physical symptoms, including slurred speech, agitated or lethargic demeanor, uncoordinated movement, and inappropriate responses to questions;

- abnormal conduct or erratic behavior while at work, or significant deterioration in work performance;
- a report of drug use provided by a reliable and credible source that has been independently corroborated;
- evidence that the employee has tampered with current drug test results;
- information that the employee has caused or contributed to an accident at work; or
- evidence that the employee has used, possessed, sold, solicited, or transferred drugs while working or at work."[69]

Consult with a legal expert prior to issuing any discipline in response to positive drug test results.

Because there are critical procedural details and legal ambiguity in some aspects of reasonable suspicion drug testing, it is best practice to consult with a legal expert prior to conducting any drug testing or when issuing any discipline in response to positive results.

If employers decide that they would like to be able to test their employees when incidents warranting reasonable suspicion arise, there are some proactive steps they should take first.

First, it is vital to have a policy prohibiting workplace intoxication and working under the influence. It may be illegal to require an employee to submit to a drug test if there was no policy or any other demonstration that the employer had put employees on notice that they may be subjected to testing under certain circumstances.

When these incidents do arise, employers must be mindful to properly follow up and address them in a timely manner, including identifying and documenting the incidents and reasons for testing. Drug testing should be required within *eight hours* for alcohol *and within thirty-two hours* for drugs.

Additionally, all supervisors should be properly trained to identify signs of drug use, document the reasons for testing, and the protocol for following up and addressing such incidents with employees.

(d) *Post-Incident Testing* – As the name indicates, post-incident testing is required drug testing of employees who were involved in workplace accidents. Post-incident testing differs from reasonable suspicion testing because it may not be readily apparent that an employee was under the influence in the accident giving rise to the testing.

Employers should be proactive by implementing strict policies and procedures for how and when post-incident testing will occur. For example, it may be when there is a fatality, injury while operating heavy machinery, incidents requiring medical attention, or damage to vehicles or property above a specified monetary amount. Similar to reasonable suspicion testing, employers should require testing within a specified amount of time from the incident. As a best practice, post-incident testing should happen within twelve hours of the incident, if not sooner, given that the duration of drugs and alcohol vary. Additionally, the employee should not return to work the same day of the testing and incident.

Post-incident testing should happen within 12 hours of the incident.

Employers should confine the testing to only those individuals whose conduct contributed to or caused the accident. It is important not to test the individual who merely reported the incident or injury, or the person who was just injured but did not contribute to the injury, otherwise, it may appear retaliatory and a means of penalizing the employee.

Handling Accommodations (Marijuana and Alcohol)

Marijuana – Despite the use of marijuana for medicinal purposes in certain states, because it is still illegal under federal law, the ADA does not provide reasonable accommodations at work for its use. Under the ADA, individuals currently using illegal drugs do not qualify as disabled individuals who are entitled to reasonable accommodations.[70] Even though the federal courts find that that there is no protection for medicinal marijuana under the ADA, an increasing number of states have recognized marijuana for legitimate medicinal purposes and provided protection through state anti-discrimination laws.[71]

Alcohol – In part because alcohol is legal and because alcoholism is recognized as a legitimate medical condition, under the ADA individuals who abuse alcohol may be considered disabled and warrant reasonable accommodations. As such, employers must provide reasonable accommodations to such qualified disabled individuals when requested or when the employer becomes aware of its necessity. How an employer becomes aware of its necessity is a sensitive issue. Because alcoholism is a qualified disability, an employer should be wary not to ask questions that might elicit whether the individual has a disability or information about the disability, which is illegal. Instead, the employer should focus any inquiries for an accommodation on the individual's subpar performance or concerns of the employee carrying out specific tasks. This does not mean, however, that an employer cannot ask about individuals' alcohol use if it is to ascertain whether they violated a company drug-use policy. Furthermore, while employers may inquire as to how they can assist or provide resources to struggling workers, employers have no duty to offer accommodations to workers who fail to request such accommodation and who deny having disabilities.[72]

Consistent Employee Standards – Despite having to make reasonable accommodations for alcoholic employees, employers can still enforce rules concerning alcohol or marijuana use in the workplace, which includes prohibiting the consumption of either, *while at work*. Also, while employers may not be able to discriminate against employees for their disabilities (and sometimes marijuana use, medicinal or otherwise), employers can still prohibit their employees from being under the influence while at work. With the exception of the reasonable accommodation for an employee, which likely entails a leave of absence if for alcoholism, an employer can hold its alcohol and marijuana using employees to the same work standards as the rest of the employees. Neither an accommodation nor otherwise gets to be an excuse for unsatisfactory performance or unacceptable behavior, even if it is related to the employee's alcoholism or marijuana use.

TIPS FOR DRAFTING DRUG AND ALCOHOL POLICIES

If employers want to test their employees for drugs, it is vital for them to have a Drug-Free Workplace policy. Employers covered by the Drug-Free Workplace Act are required to have a policy provided to all employees informing them that drug use is a violation of the company policy. Even for employers not covered by the act, many states require that they already have a written policy explicitly stating the expectation of maintaining a drug-free workforce and that employees may be subject to drug tests, in order for the employer to test them. A drug-free policy should not merely state that drug use is not allowed, it should identify which workers (positions) are covered under the policy, and explain the circumstances for different tests, the testing procedures, and the consequences for refusal to submit within identified timeframes. As a best practice, employers should consider including the following sections:

(a) **Consequences** – The policy should clearly state what the potential consequences may be for failing an examination. For applicants, a positive drug test result will likely result in revoking the employment offer. For current employees, employers should consider what type of discipline should be expected. Will employees be granted one free pass, be allowed to retest, or be subject to some form of discipline? If so, would it be immediate termination or predetermined levels of progressive discipline? Do they immediately lose their rights to continue working in their positions until they test negative? These are all questions employers should consider answering in their policies.

(b) **Tested Substances** – It is important for the policy to explicitly list which substances the examination will be testing for.

For conditionally offered applicants, employers should confine the examination to testing the commonly used 4/5-panel drug test. This test is used by the federal government and checks for illegal substances, including cocaine, amphetamine/methamphetamine, opiates, PCP, and THC.[73] It is called the common 4/5-panel test because, in response to the developing legal landscape, many employers are now tweaking the typical 5-panel test by declining to screen for THC, given recent laws in some states providing certain protections for marijuana users in the employment context. Additionally, the

ADA prohibits employers from gathering medical information. As such, it is best to confine the pre-hire examination to testing for only illegal substances, and not alcohol, as an alcoholic may be recognized as disabled under the ADA.

However, for current employees, a more robust examination may be used, such as the commonly used 7-panel drug test that also tests for excessive use of prescription drugs. The 7-panel test can be used with current employees and tests for marijuana, cocaine, opiates, PCP, amphetamines, benzodiazepines, and barbiturates.[74] This test is commonly used by employers when alertness is required, or heavy machinery is operated, and there is a strong safety rationale to test for prescription drugs with potentially fatiguing side effects. While these prescription drugs may be legal, if abused they could significantly impair an employee's ability to carry out tasks and responsibilities that may be vital to safety or business operations, e.g., operating heavy machinery or medical operations.

As a best practice, employers should refrain from testing for prescription drugs, unless required to. Testing for legal medications could potentially create substantial liability exposure. To test for legal medications, the employer needs to individually assess each positive for how it could affect employees in carrying out their job duties. Additionally, testing for certain medications may indicate that an employee has a disability, which raises ADA issues.

(c) **Collection Method** – It is important that the policy clearly state what collection method will be used for the drug test, e.g., urine, breath, hair, etc. The most commonly accepted collection method has been a urine sample. This method is widely accepted and approved by the federal government. Additionally, it can detect drug use within the last two to four days.

(d) **Who Conducts the Test** – Whenever possible, it is a best practice to have a reputable third-party, off-site company conduct the examination. Drug testing with long-standing or credible third-party agencies can protect the employer from lawsuits alleging bias and targeting (tampering with results) and against claims of inaccurate testing procedures. Third-party sites have trained professionals who are removed from the employer's day-to-day operations and who routinely conduct such examinations from the collection process to the laboratory analysis.

(e) **Consistency for All Employees Within the Same Position** – The drug-free policy must be consistently applied, not only choosing who must be tested but also what disciplinary measures will be issued for failed results. If a certain classification is tested, especially due to it having safety considerations, then all employees operating in that position and handling the same body of work should also be tested. Employers cannot be selective in who they require to submit to testing. If certain reasons are given for testing one individual, that same rationale should be consistently applied to all employees to which that reason is applicable. The employer should identify the specific job duties or tasks in the job descriptions that imply a drug-free necessity.

(f) **Consistency Among Policies** – Employers should be consistent with their drug-free policies in all places that refer to them, such as the Drug-Free Workplace and Drug Testing Policy, the handbook policy acknowledgment and disclaimer, any statements in job advertisements, and in interviews. Contrasting policies can potentially invalidate each other if ever legally challenged.

(g) **Confidentiality** – Employers should be sure to state in the policy that the company shall keep all information associated with or resulting from the testing confidential. As a best practice, employers should treat all drug tests like medical information by implementing the same confidentiality practices. Such practices may include storing all test results in a file separate from employment files, limiting access to test results, or not allowing information associated with the tests to be sent out on a common area fax machine or on an unrestricted computer.

Off-Duty Behavior and Social Media

Employees are generally allowed to conduct themselves as they wish outside the workplace without concerns of it implicating their employment. However, under certain circumstances, actions outside of the workplace can still violate a workplace policy and warrant discipline. Employment may be implicated if an employee's actions create a workplace concern.

When Addressing Off-Duty Conduct Is Appropriate

Generally, there must be a direct nexus between the off-duty conduct and the employment. Arbitration precedent under the National Labor Relations Act tends to focus on whether the alleged off-duty misconduct

1. has a connection or nexus with the employee's work,
2. resulted in actual harm to the employer,
3. violated a company policy or the contractual relationship, or
4. was done with malice or knowledge that the employer would suffer harm.[75]

Common examples of off-duty behavior that create workplace concerns include employees threatening and harassing other employees, publicly disparaging the employer, and exposing confidential employment matters.

In addition, employees' positions may have legal regulations that can be affected by their off-duty conduct. For example, an employee convicted of a violent act may be prevented from working in a position with supervisory authority over minors due to federal or state law. In such circumstances, the employer has an obligation to take particular remedial action in response to the employee's off-duty conduct.

Investigation Scope of Off-Duty Complaints

After it has been determined that there is a strong nexus between the alleged misconduct and the workplace, the employer may initiate an investigation into the allegation and determine the scope of the investigation. An investigation into off-duty conduct should be conducted in the same way a workplace complaint would be investigated, such as investigating the complainant, the accused, and any witnesses. The only real difference is that there are privacy concerns to be mindful of. (For additional discussion on conducting investigations, see "How to Investigate Misconduct" on page 114). Taking into consideration these concerns, the scope of the investigation should be confined to public information and witness testimony. The employer should never allow the investigation scope to expand so broadly as to include private or confidential matters, especially when there is no connection to the workplace. The employer is not a private investigator, and it is the employer's duty to dictate the scope of the investigation.

The employer should never allow the investigation scope to expand so broadly as to include private or confidential matters, especially when there is no connection to the workplace.

The same rationale applies when investigating matters implicating social media. Whenever possible, it is best to confine the scope of any investigatory work to information that is publicly accessible.

Social Media

A rapidly growing issue regarding off-duty misconduct involves the use of social media. Employers should make it clear to employees that social media use, similar to other off-duty conduct, may be actionable and result in discipline.

There are two options to create a workplace policy that notifies employees of the expectations regarding social media usage. The first is to have an explicit social media policy that addresses all potential misconduct that may need to be addressed by the employer. The second option is to include a statement in the workplace standard of conduct that notifies employees that the policies include all off-duty behavior and social media use that may impact the workplace and be in violation of the policies' standards. If there already is a strong misconduct policy in place, make it clear that the policy also includes off-duty behavior and social media.

Employers should never friend request, follow, or attempt to connect with employees on social media.

In a growing number of states, there are laws protecting individuals' privacy rights, particularly as they relate to social media. For example, in Washington State, employers cannot ask current employees or applicants for their social media login information. Additionally, they cannot require employees to grant access to view their social media pages or profiles. As a best practice, employers (including management and HR) should never friend request, follow, or attempt to connect with employees in any form on social media. For further reading on social media regulations, see "Additional Information" at the end of the chapter (page 147).[76]

TIPS ON ADDRESSING OFF-DUTY MISCONDUCT AND SOCIAL MEDIA

1. Have a policy in place that notifies employees that their off-duty actions may be subject to discipline if they impact their employment.
2. Before initiating an investigation into off-duty action, determine whether there is a nexus between the conduct and the employment.
3. Understand applicable laws protecting employees' privacy rights, particularly as they relate to social media.
4. Never allow an investigation's scope to expand so broadly as to include private or confidential matters, including social media, especially when there is no connection to the workplace.
5. Don't friend request, follow, or attempt to connect with employees in any form on social media.

Additional Information

- List of States Enacting Workplace Anti-Bullying Laws – **Workplace Bullying Institute**, "The Healthy Workplace Bill," https://healthyworkplacebill.org/states/.
- Various State Specific Anti-discrimination Laws – **NOLO**, "Employment Discrimination in Your State," https://www.nolo.com/legal-encyclopedia/employment-discrimination-in-your-state-31017.html.
- Employer Responsibilities Under OSHA – DOL, **Occupational Safety and Health Administration**, "Employer Responsibilities," https://www.osha.gov/as/opa/worker/employer-responsibility.html.
- Information Regarding State Pre-Employment Drug Testing Laws – **Paycor, Resource Center**, "Pre-Employment Drug Testing Laws by State," https://www.paycor.com/resource-center/pre-employment-drug-testing-laws-by-state.
- States' Laws on Employee Drug Testing – **ACLU**, "State-by-State Workplace Drug Testing Laws," https://www.aclu.org/other/state-state-workplace-drug-testing-laws.
- States' Marijuana Laws – **NORML**, "Marijuana Law Reform," https://norml.org/states.
- State Protections Restricting Employer Access to Employees' Social Media – **National Conference of State Legislatures**, "State Social Media Privacy Laws," http://www.ncsl.org/research/telecommunications-and-information-technology/state-laws-prohibiting-access-to-social-media-usernames-and-passwords.aspx.
- EEOC Guidelines for an Effective Investigation Process – **U.S. Equal Employment Opportunity Commission**, "Enforcement Guidance on

Vicarious Employer Liability for Unlawful Harassment by Supervisors, Section V(C)(1), Policy and Complaint Procedure," https://www.eeoc.gov/policy/docs/harassment.html.

- EEOC Guidelines for Preventing and Addressing Misconduct and Employer Responsibilities – **EEOC**, "Enforcement Guidance on Vicarious Employer Liability for Unlawful Harassment by Supervisors, Section V(C)(2)-(3), Other Preventive and Corrective Measures and Small Businesses," https://www.eeoc.gov/policy/docs/harassment.html.

Discipline, Discharge, and Documentation

5

A report by Workplace Bullying Institute found that 72 percent of workers believe that their employers inadequately handled workplace bullying that they knew about, including "doing nothing after a complaint was filed" (26 percent) and "conducting an inadequate investigation with nothing changing" (46 percent). Furthermore, it claims, "Employers have the power to either sustain or eliminate abusive conduct. Anecdotal evidence suggests that American employers rarely take steps to assist the aggrieved employee," and "in 54 percent of cases, bullying stops only when the target loses her or his job."[77]

When to Consider Discipline and at What Level

Even after an investigation is concluded and allegations of misconduct are substantiated or determined to have more than likely occurred, the employer's duty is not over; the disruptive employee's behavior must still be addressed. The law requires the employer to take corrective action when aware of certain misconduct, such as sexual harassment or actions creating a hostile work environment. Remediating a situation and taking corrective action in the workplace usually takes the form of discipline, transfer, termination, or submitting to a rehabilitative employment program, if available, such as an employee assistance program. Even without a legal obligation, employers should try and prevent misconduct from occurring, and respond appropriately when it does occur.

Discipline should be used as a tool to correct or rehabilitate the employee's behavior.

When deciding whether to issue some form of discipline to an employee, it is first important to consider discipline as a tool that should be used to correct or rehabilitate the employee's behavior, and not to penalize or punish. When employers issue discipline that appears to be punitive and to penalize employees for their mistakes, they fail to rehabilitate those employees because even if they do improve, they do so in response to fear; fear of losing their jobs or enduring greater hardship at the hands of their employers. Overly-severe discipline decreases workplace morale in the long-run; impacts retention, as it undermines job security; and affects productivity, as employees feel undervalued.

Whenever discipline is issued to an employee, it should be reflective of the severity of the violation. When judging the severity of an action, as a guide, employers should consider whether there (a) was malice on behalf of the employee, (b) is a continuous pattern of misbehavior, and (c) was harm caused to the employer.

Levels of Discipline. Generally, the various levels of discipline employers consider issuing are verbal warnings, written reprimands, suspension (of various durations), demotion, and termination.

The "Just Cause" Legal Standard

It is important for employers to be aware of what the legal standards are regarding termination. First, employees who are at will can be discharged for any reason or no reason at all, as long as it is not discriminatory. Employees who are nonexempt and protected by a contract with a separation clause are usually held to a just-cause standard, meaning that the employer may only terminate the employee if just cause can be established.

Just cause is a legal term of art that comprises multiple factors, created through years of case precedent:

Laws to Know

1. *Reasonable Rule* – Is the rule or order reasonably related to the orderly, efficient, and safe operation of the business?

2. *Prior Notice* – Did the employee receive adequate notice of the work rule or performance standard and the possible consequences for failing to comply?

3. *Fair Investigation* – Was the investigation fair, unbiased, and objective?
4. *Thorough Investigation* – Did the employer investigate before deciding to impose discipline?
5. *Proof* – Was there proof or evidence of the violation to support the misconduct or performance discrepancy?
6. *Equal Treatment* – Have other employees been dealt with equally for the same or similar actions?
7. *Appropriate Penalty* – Does the discipline imposed appropriately reflect the severity of the violation?[78]

Progressive Discipline

When determining whether a particular level of discipline is appropriate, the employer should consider whether progressive discipline has been satisfied. Progressive discipline is a system in which the severity of discipline increases for repeat occurrences. For example, progressive discipline would not be satisfied if an employer decided to terminate an employee for being five minutes late to work the first or second time. Progressive discipline would have the employer gradually increase the severity of discipline for repeat occurrences of tardiness, such as a warning, reprimand, suspension, and then termination.

Lack of progressive discipline can be an argument alleging that the employer did not have just cause to issue a termination. Progressive discipline can be a component of the appropriate penalty factor of just cause. Although, as mentioned, for at-will employees, just cause is not needed to terminate an employee.

Regardless, discipline for egregious actions generally never needs to satisfy progressive discipline. An egregious violation would be one of malice on the part of the employee, such as theft or violence, or an act that causes substantial harm to the employer, such as fraud. An employer would not need to demonstrate that the employee has first been warned or given a written reprimand for punching a supervisor or embezzling thousands of dollars; the natural response would likely be termination, short of extreme mitigating circumstances.

Liability Assessment Check

While meeting legal standards is one thing employers should consider when making personnel decisions, such as issuing discipline, it is also important to assess whether the decision is solely based on an impartial legitimate business rationale or one's own predispositions and personal bias. It may be difficult to assess one's own biases, but this is an issue that employers must consider. Having a tool, such as a checklist,

Employers should assess whether a personnel decision is based on an impartial legitimate business rationale or one's own predispositions and personal bias.

to help assess implicit bias for decisions having a disparate impact on workers, is important for all employers, especially those organizations who claim to truly value being model equal opportunity employers. Simply calling yourself one, while making business decisions with a detrimental impact to an already marginalized group of workers, does not make for an equal opportunity employer in practice. Additionally, having a tool to assess unintentional racism has a bottom-line benefit: it will help prevent and defend against discrimination lawsuits.

Employers should use checklists to assess for implicit bias.

An employer should consider the following prior to making any personnel decisions, especially termination:

(a) Assess whether the personnel decision is based on the employee's individual performance or based on an assumption related to that employee's belonging to a protected classification, such as gender, ethnicity, age, disability, religion, etc.

(b) Is there a substantive business rationale or need associated with the decision? If so, is this rationale or basis documented and consistent with established company policies and practices?

(c) When personnel decisions are in contrast to company policies or practices, it is generally a good idea to hire a professional consultant who can help determine whether the decision creates liability exposure and, if so, the best way to minimize it.

(d) When performance issues are involved, it is always best to document all attempts to assist the employee to improve, the employee's failure to meet expectations, and all notices to the employee of substandard performance. Prior to seeking discharge for an employee with consistent minor performance issues, it is best to issue remedial tools designed to assist and document performance, such as a performance improvement plan, which is not disciplinary, yet helps satisfy progressive discipline concerns. For additional discussion on performance improvement plans, refer to the later section, "Essential Documentation for Discipline and Discharge; Performance Improvement Plan" (page 162).

When personnel decisions are in contrast to company policies or practices, it is generally a good idea to hire a professional consultant who can help determine whether the decision creates liability exposure and, if so, the best way to minimize it.

(e) When relaying feedback to employees, whether informally (e.g., a casual conversation during lunch) or formally (e.g., an annual performance evaluation), it is important to be accurate and straightforward, regardless of whether it is praise or criticism. Giving employees satisfactory feedback when it does not accurately reflect their work may create other issues in the future, especially if discipline, including termination, is necessary. For additional discussion on performance feedback, refer to later section, "Essential Documentation for Discipline and Discharge; Performance Evaluations" (page 169).

(f) Explanations given for personnel decisions, whether verbally or in writing, should be consistent with the documented feedback the employee receives. It is a good practice for the personnel decision to be consistent with the next step of progressive discipline, if the decision is disciplinary in nature, e.g., a demotion or termination.

(g) Employers should check that all personnel decisions are consistent with the treatment of other employees. Two questions to ask are, (1) Have other employees been disciplined just as severely for the same offense? (2) What offenses have others committed who have received this same level of discipline, and were those actions just as severe as the offense being considered now?

TIPS TO MINIMIZE LIABILITY BEFORE, DURING, AND AFTER DISCHARGE

Navigating the legal landmines can feel daunting, unclear, and overwhelming, especially when considering discharging an employee and worrying about a wrongful termination lawsuit. Despite the various legal conundrums an employer may face, there are precautions employers can take immediately to mitigate legal exposure and best practices to protect themselves in the future.

Here are four common liability mitigating tactics any employer can implement today:

1. *Documentation.* Proper documentation is likely one of the most important practices all employers should strive to maintain to protect themselves from liability regrading employment-related decisions. The employer's documentation of a situation tends to become the crux of most workplace-related lawsuits, especially with matters related to termination or discipline.

It is vital that employers understand the importance of paper trails and how to properly leave them. Documented circumstances tend to be the most legally persuasive, and unfortunately, when an incident isn't properly captured in writing, it typically is held against the employer's position, not the employees'.

A proper paper trail should capture that the employee was put on notice of the expectation (typically a signed employee or personnel policy handbook satisfies this burden). Additionally, paper trails should include employees' being explicitly put on notice that their actions or performance were falling short of standards and expectations, and that if subpar performance continued that they could be subject to discipline, including what that discipline may be. If employees have legitimate justifications as to why they are substandard, it is important to document those as well, and whether they constitute legitimate justifications or whether there is an expectation for working around such excuses.

It is important that any feedback the employee receives be consistent and accurate. Giving inaccurate performance feedback, whether good or bad, only creates additional liability exposure. Especially when addressing terminations, it is vital that the reasons for the termination are accurately documented and clearly communicated at the time of the termination.

Additionally, it is important that whatever policies are being identified as establishing the expectations are consistently applied to other employees as well.

2. *Same Decision Maker.* Another tactic employers can use to protect themselves when handling terminations is to have one individual handle the hiring and firing for certain positions or workgroups within the organization. Designating one individual in HR as the hiring/firing decision maker for the majority of positions mitigates the possibility of the appearance that a particular employee or manager has pushed someone out for personal reasons or that inconsistent explanations are communicated to the employee being let go, thus creating liability exposure. Additionally, it is not uncommon for courts to dismiss cases of wrongful termination under the "same actor doctrine," when the same individual who hired the employee also was the one who made the decision to terminate the employee. Under this defense, the theory is that the individual who hired the employee of a protected class likely would not suddenly develop an aversion to that protected class and decide to fire that employee on a discriminatory basis.

As such, whenever possible, organizations should attempt to designate a single decision maker for the ultimate hiring and firing decisions for particular positions and workgroups.

3. *Replacement Defense.* A persuasive tactic employers can use when concerned about a claim for wrongful termination based on a separating employee's protected class is to hire as a replacement someone who is in the same protected class. Courts will generally be willing to dismiss a lawsuit for wrongful termination based on a protected class (i.e., race, religion, national origin, sex, etc.) if the replacement hired also belongs to that class. This demonstrates that it was the employee's performance and conduct, as opposed to the employee's protected status, that gave rise to the termination.

4. *Equal Enforcement of Policies.* Simply substantiating that an employee violated a known policy or expectation is often not enough to protect an employer from a wrongful termination lawsuit; it must also be established that all such actions are equally enforced and responded to in a consistent manner. As such, it is vital for employers to demonstrate that they are equally enforcing their policies

against employees and responding in a consistent manner. Specifically, employers should issue similar levels of discipline to employees for similar violations. Furthermore, the severity of the discipline should match the egregiousness of the violation. Terminating an employee for minor offenses, such as tardiness, could invite a lawsuit if other employees were disciplined far less severely for far more egregious actions. As such, employers should prioritize documenting all feedback given to employees regarding performance and maintain complete documentation in employees' personnel files.

Essential Documentation for Discipline and Discharge

Document. Document. Document. "Lack of solid documentation is the single most common mistake employers make when handling discipline or terminations. Good records, on the other hand, can mean the difference between winning and losing a lawsuit."[79]

Performance Improvement Plan

Performance Improvement Plans (PIPs) are exactly what they sound like, a formal process used by employers to track and measure employees' work and performance in their positions over a period of time. PIPs can be used to address employees' deficiencies, whether regarding performance, results, or even behavior-related concerns. These can be excellent tools for working with employees on addressing their deficiencies and providing consistent feedback and assistance to help them be successful or identify why it is that they are unable to be.

PIPs do not need to be considered a form of discipline. They are an alternative to taking actual discipline that may affect employees' paychecks, such as a demotion, suspension, or even termination. PIPs can be seen as a corrective tool that employees can rely on for specific and measurable goals on exactly what they need to do to be successful in their positions.

When a PIP is being considered, employers need to know how to (1) determine whether a PIP is the appropriate action for the situation, (2) draft a good PIP that will help the employee succeed, (3) review that plan and remove any bias from it, (4) implement the plan effectively, (5) monitor the plan as it progresses, and (6) wrap the plan up at its conclusion.

The Society of Human Resource Management (SHRM) has put together a brief yet thorough summary addressing each of these concerns that may help employers understand how to establish a performance improvement plan.[80] SHRM recommends the following when considering a PIP.

Step 1: Determine if a PIP Is Appropriate

A PIP should be used when there is a commitment to help the employee improve, not as a way for a frustrated manager to start the termination process. Used as the latter, it's nothing more than a document trail that should already exist, and it signifies to all employees that no such help is available. Bottom line: HR needs to assess if a structured plan with time-sensitive goals is the appropriate next step, or if a PIP will be more of a detriment than an aid.

To assess whether a PIP is warranted, HR should consider the following:

- Is there an actual performance or behavioral issue that can be substantiated? Ask the manager to create a list of the performance deficiencies, including dates, specific data or detailed explanations, and any previous guidance given to the employee. Review the most recent performance appraisal to see if the issue is new or ongoing. Has the manager met expectations to prevent the need for a PIP?
- Do you feel the manager is committed to helping the employee succeed, or is his or her intention focused on terminating the employee? This can

be tricky to assess, but listen for whether the manager is concerned about the employee and wants to help, or if he or she is at the end of their rope and no longer able to manage the situation. Insecure managers may feel threatened by some employee's behaviors or may not understand that managing includes supporting and developing employees. If the manager doesn't want employees to succeed, there is little point in starting a PIP.

- Is it likely that the issue can be "fixed" through a formal improvement plan? Problems with sales goals, quality ratings, quantity objectives and similar issues may be well-suited to a structured plan that helps identify why the deficiencies occur. Insubordinate and insolent behaviors, on the other hand, might not lend themselves to improvement using the goal-oriented process of a PIP.

- Does it appear the employee has received proper training to succeed at the task? A leave of absence or other time off may have resulted in missed training or informative meetings that were not later made available to the employee. Additional training may be warranted to correct the oversight.

- Is there a known personal issue that may be affecting the employee's performance? When personal difficulties strike, employees may have a dip in performance that employers often accommodate. If the reasonable time frame for accommodation has ended, a PIP may serve to help a capable employee get refocused and back on track.

Step 2: Develop a Draft Plan

Once the need for a PIP has been established, have the manager create a draft of the plan for HR to review. An improvement plan should include:

- Information on what acceptable performance levels are and how the employee's current performance is deficient. Specifics regarding the unacceptable performance should be given, including dates, data and detailed explanations. Attach the job description and any relevant employer policies to further clarify expectations.
- Specific and measurable objectives that are achievable, relevant and time-bound (otherwise known as SMART goals). PIPs usually last 30, 60 or 90 days, depending on how long it would reasonably take to improve the specific issue. Examples might be:
  - *In May, June and July, Jane Smith's quality errors must not exceed 3 percent each month,*

and she must produce at least 150 units each month.

- *During this 90-day performance evaluation, John Smith must have perfect attendance, with the exception of approved medical or family absences. This means that he must clock in and be ready for work by the start of each scheduled shift, return from all scheduled breaks on time and remain at work for his entire shift.*

- Guidance on what management will do or provide to assist the employee in achieving these goals, such as additional resources, training or coaching.
- Details on how often the manager and employee will meet to discuss progress. This is often done once a week, but may vary depending on the circumstances.
- Clearly stated consequences for not meeting the objectives of the plan. Options may include demotion, transfer to a different position or termination.

Step 3: Review the Plan

HR should review the plan with a focus on removing any bias against the employee. Is the performance issue clearly stated and well-substantiated? Are the objectives fair and the time frames reasonable? For example, is a salesperson given a sales goal that far surpasses the projected sales of the clients assigned? Is the employee being given the proper tools and training needed to improve? If it's a relatively new employee, was an adequate onboarding effort in place to help the employee become acclimated? If HR has a role in making those provisions, that process should start immediately. The key to this step is to ensure that the plan is attainable and fair and not just a means to terminate an employee.

Step 4: Implement the Plan

It's time to meet with the employee to discuss the plan and expectations. While not the most pleasant of meetings, it helps if the manager conveys his or her own commitment to the plan and to the employee's success. Employee feedback should be encouraged to help identify areas of confusion and to help foster ownership. Be open to changes based on the employee's input; the perspective of a valued employee (one worth the time and effort of a PIP), is no less valuable here and may lead to a more effective plan.

After fully discussing the plan, the manager may make modifications based on employee feedback. Once HR has reviewed any changes, the final plan should be signed by both manager and employee and forwarded to HR for approval.

If the employee is unable to commit to the PIP process at this point, the employer will need to determine whether termination, demotion or another appropriate employment action should be taken.

Step 5: Monitor Plan Progression

The manager should ensure all progress meetings are scheduled and occur on time. Cancelling meetings or showing up late would convey a lack of importance and commitment on the manager's part. Progress toward goals should be documented and discussed, seeking to identify why improvements have or have not been made. If gaps in training or required tools become apparent, provide those as soon as possible. Encourage employees to lead these meetings, to self-report on how they believe they are doing and what realizations they might have made, or what else they feel they need to succeed.

Successful progress made toward the goal should be recognized as a means of motivating the employee to continued improvement.

Step 6: Plan Conclusion

When the employee has responded positively by meeting plan objectives, possibly before the expiration date of the plan, the employer should formally close the PIP, recognize the employee's success and allow the employee to continue employment. While a positive occasion for the employee, the manager must be sure the employee understands that continued good performance is expected.

If an employee is unable to improve or if his or her performance worsens, the PIP should be closed, and a possible reassignment, demotion or termination should be considered, based on the specific circumstances.

When the employee is committed to improvement, but falls short of the objectives within the established timeline, it may be worthwhile to extend the plan to give him or her a bit more time to succeed. Additionally, if objectives were found, in retrospect, to not be realistic or fully within the employee's control, the plan might be ended successfully, based on the improvements achieved.

Performance Evaluations

Purpose of Performance Evaluations

A performance evaluation is a constructive tool to be used by the employer to relay specific and documented feedback on an employee's performance over a period of time. By giving consistent evaluations, the employer ensures that its employees are aware of expectations and how their performance is viewed by management. It is also an opportunity to acknowledge workers who have excelled and reward them for their accomplishments.

Clear Expectations

Prior to conducting evaluations, it is vital that the employer be clear what the performance standards and expectations are of the employee. Performance standards are the essential functions of the position. These standards should be reflective of the position's duties as stated in the job description, which makes sense, since you want to measure the employee based on the position's expectations for which they applied and were hired. These standards are specific to the position and not the person. Meaning, any employee working in this position should be held to the same standards. Contrarily, while standards are based on the position, goals are tailored to the individual employee and not just the position. Employee goals, which should also always be a component of the evaluation, address individual strengths and weaknesses, including personality issues and communication styles, among others, if identified as areas needing improvement.

While standards are based on the position, goals are tailored to the individual employee and not just the position.

Tracking Performance and Constant Feedback

Performance evaluations should provide specific feedback, with examples of the employee's performance supporting each mark. In order to do this, the employer must adequately track the employee's performance. It is important to note memorable incidents, projects, issues, and concerns, both good and bad, as they come up. Feedback for these incidents should not be withheld; they should be relayed to the employee when they happen, or sometime soon after. Any discussions on improving, like a coaching and counseling meeting, should be memorialized and documented in a file, preferably the employee's personnel file. This file and the feedback given in the evaluation should not be a surprise to the employee. This is why it is important for the employer to give frequent feedback of an employee's performance and not wait for an evaluation. By giving constant feedback and documenting it, an employer is also protecting itself in the event that it must discipline the employee for performance deficiencies that the employee challenges.

> *It is important to note memorable incidents, projects, issues, and concerns, both good and bad, as they come up. Feedback for these incidents should not be withheld; they should be relayed to the employee when they happen, or sometime soon after.*

Preparing and Conducting Performance Evaluations

Performance evaluations should be conducted on a consistent basis, at least once a year. These performance evaluations must be conducted with *all* employees to prevent the appearance that particular employees are being unfairly targeted for harassment.

It is important to prepare for the evaluation prior to meeting with the employee. To prepare, the evaluator should gather all relevant materials (i.e., the employee's personnel file, a supervisor's file, any documented incidents, emails, etc.) and review all documents and records relating to the employee's performance, productivity, and behavior. It is a good practice to have the evaluation written out with all supporting documentation on hand prior to the meeting. When completing the evaluation, the employer should review each standard and goal set for that employee, clearly state on the evaluation document the employer's conclusion as to whether the employee has met the standard or goal, and have clear reasons for each mark, with the supporting evidence if negative.

When conducting the evaluation with the employee, it is important to be candid and clear. This is not a meeting to be vague, generalize, or beat around the bush. While this meeting is an opportunity to have a discussion on areas the employee needs to improve, it is also an opportunity to give appreciation for areas in which the employee excels. Clearly explain conclusions point by point and don't give general or boilerplate explanations for marks. These meetings are meant to be discussions, and the employer should solicit the employee's feedback and note it. Additionally, it is important that the employee be allowed to follow up after the conclusion of the evaluation to give feedback or draft a rebuttal to the evaluation and possibly have it attached to the evaluation and placed in their personnel file.

TIPS FOR CONDUCTING PERFORMANCE EVALUATIONS

1. When setting goals and standards, be specific and use objective measures.
2. Set deadlines when giving tasks and objectives.
3. Be realistic by setting achievable goals.
4. When giving feedback be honest, whether it be good or bad. Exaggerating an employee's contributions, accomplishments, or deficiencies can create legal issues in the future, especially in situations where the employer must issue discipline due to performance.
5. Evaluate the employee's performance, not personality. If there is a concern that involves the employee's personality, when relaying feedback focus on how personality and character impact the business and the employee's performance.
6. Be sure to listen to the employee's feedback and consider including that input in the evaluation. This will help the process, foster collaboration, and improve relations between management and employees.

Separation Agreements

What Is a Separation and Release Agreement?

An employment separation agreement, also known as a release agreement, is a written contract between an employer and an employee outlining the terms of the employee's separation. Most commonly, separation agreements include a payout to the departing employee in exchange for the employee's waiving the right to file claims against the employer. Typically, this agreement is broken up into two parts.

It is important to note that the EEOC's position is that covenants not to file administrative charges are not enforceable. As such, it is a good idea to draft the release so that it waives the separating employee's right to recover monetary damages for any administrative charges.

The first is the employee's waiver of rights to bring a legal claim against the employer. Usually this is a general release of common legal claims arising from employment, such as employment law claims, compensation claims, discrimination claims, and claims for attorney fees and costs. It is important to note that the EEOC's position is that covenants not to file administrative charges are not enforceable. As such, it is a good idea to draft the release so that it waives the separating employee's right to recover monetary damages for any administrative charges. While this may not prevent the employee from filing charges in and of itself, it is a substantial deterrent, given that it would remove any financial incentive or motive a separating employee may have to file charges.

The second part of a separation agreement is the fee the employee receives in exchange for the waiver to claims. Because some employment contracts already dictate an employee's severance upon separation, the fee an employee receives for signing the release is not always the severance package itself, but an additional amount. The agreement usually includes other provisions, which may include severance.

When to Pursue a Separation Agreement

Offering severance in exchange for a release can be a great tool for employers to avoid the risk of a lawsuit; mitigating liability should be a priority for any employer. However, this does not mean that every departing employee should be offered severance in exchange for a separation agreement. It may not be economically wise.

There are no laws that require employers to offer severance, even when laying off employees. In circumstances in which an employee is being terminated for extreme misconduct, employers generally should forego offering severance so as to not appear as if they are rewarding inappropriate conduct. Other employees, who may be considering departing for personal reasons, may see that as an excuse to act out and get paid for it as their means for separating. However, when terminations are merely for poor performance, employers should assess these situations on a case-by-case basis. They should weigh (1) how the bad the performance was; (2) whether the employees are "high-risk" because, perhaps, they recently raised harassment or discrimination claims, or because the employer did a poor job assisting or documenting employee performance; and (3) the longevity of their employment, as long-service employees create greater liability exposure.

Additionally, severance should be used if the employer wishes to have the employee agree to any post-employment restraints, such as a confidentiality clause, non-disparagement clause, noncompete, or otherwise. If these are not agreed to at the initial hiring of the employee, the employer may be required to offer consideration to the employee, i.e., severance.

Drafting a Separation Agreement

When drafting a separation agreement, it is best to consult with a legal expert. Separation agreements should be drafted much more stringently than most other contracts. When challenged, separation agreements are heavily scrutinized by the court in favor of the employee, given the disproportionate bargaining power employers have when entering into such agreements.

When challenged, separation agreements are heavily scrutinized by the court in favor of the employee, given the disproportionate bargaining power employers have when entering into such agreements

Additionally, each state has its own applicable laws regarding separation agreements that should be reviewed prior to executing. There are also some federal regulations that touch on aspects of an employment separation agreement that can be used to challenge the contract's validity, e.g., FLSA, FMLA, ADEA, and state workers' compensation claim laws (for more information on applicable laws potentially challenging a separation agreement's validity, see "Additional Information" at the end of the chapter on page 187).

Furthermore, employers should be mindful when coming to an agreement with an employee that there are no surrounding circumstances to challenge or undermine the voluntariness of the agreement, such as incapacity, coercion, etc.

Common provisions contained within separation agreements include:

(a) *Details of Separation* – This part of the agreement may include the characterization of the separation (layoff, resignation, termination) or maintain neutrality and simply state, "The employee has left the company."

(b) *Severance* – Some agreements may include severance packages, although these are not required and do not have to include a monetary payout. Even during layoffs, it is a common misconception that employers are obligated to include severance. The law only requires that employees be paid for all hours worked, including the last final working day, and any accrued vacation pay.

(c) *Amount and Method of Delivery* – If there is an agreement for some form of monetary payout to the employee, the agreement must spell out the exact amount and nature of the compensation. Whether the agreement includes a lump sum payout or a structured plan, the agreement should stipulate the date and delivery method.

(d) *Noncompete* – If an employer is concerned about the separating employee going to a competitor or wants to protect its interests, one tool to do this is a noncompete provision. This can restrict the separating employee from working in the same field or industry, within a geographic region, for a set duration of time. If this was not agreed to at the onset of the employee's hiring, the employer may be required to offer severance as consideration. Alternatively, if an employee has signed a noncompete at the onset of employment, part of the separation agreement could be a release from this covenant. Additional information on noncompetes and other restrictive covenants is available in the chapter, Employee Onboarding, under "How to Protect Your Customer Base and Proprietary Business Information" (page 31).

(e) *Confidentiality/Nondisclosure* – Another common provision employers tend to include to protect their interests with separating employees is a confidentiality clause in the separation agreement. A confidentiality clause or nondisclosure agreement can list specific employer-related matters that are to remain private, such as trade secrets, company finances, customer lists, and so on. This section must explicitly list those individuals who may be exceptions to this clause, such as attorneys, spouses, accountants, etc.

(f) *Non-disparagement* – A non-disparagement clause dictates what the separating employee can and cannot disclose about the employer, its employment practices, and reasons for the separation. They restrict the employee from speaking negatively or disparaging the employer's reputation and vice versa. This section may also include an agreement to sanitize the employee's personnel file by removing all negative and adverse references there may be.

(g) *Tax and Insurance* – A provision should be included that outlines the tax deductions and payment policy. It is not uncommon that, in certain cases, the employer will agree to continue paying into the employee's health insurance plan. These agreements should be explicitly spelled out.

(h) *Other Clauses* – Other provisions of the separation and release agreement that may be included are references, post-employment cooperation, an integration clause, the return of company property, and a rehiring policy.

Tips for Drafting Separation Agreements

Once employers decide that a separation agreement may be needed or sought out with a separating employee, they should ensure that the agreement

1. is drafted clearly, with plain language known in that industry;
2. explicitly refers to the employee's rights under the ADEA if the separating employee is forty years old or older;
3. states that the employer has no obligation to rehire the employee, if applicable;
4. states that the separating employee is not waiving future rights or claims;
5. keeps the covenants not to sue and the employee's waiver of rights separate within the

agreement, as they are independent concepts and restrictions that should not be confused;

6. advises the employee in writing to hire an independent attorney to review the agreement prior to executing;
7. explicitly states that the employee is not waiving the right to file a complaint with an administrative agency or participate in an investigation, but that is relinquishing the right to collect monetary damages if an administrative complaint is pursued;
8. does not require the employee to return any severance received if an administrative charge is filed, but instead designates that such amount is to be deducted from any monetary damages collected, if applicable; and
9. allows the employee twenty-one days to consider the agreement and another seven days after executing the agreement for the employee to revoke it, only at which point should the agreement go into effect (this is in accordance with the ADEA, for employees forty years or older).

Employee Offboarding

> *"With the rise of social media and employees' ability to openly critique their [current and prior] employers on the Internet, everyone is now a potential target for bad press and critical reviews."*[81]

Not all separations are for negative reasons or on bad terms. While having good employees leave is never something an employer wants, there are many times when employees leave for reasons unrelated to the job itself, and these incidents can be used as opportunities for employers to demonstrate that they value their employees, even those leaving. Employers should have plans in place to address separating employees.

Once notified by an employee of their intention to depart, there are a few phases an employer must consider and address. First, there are a few immediate concerns that the employer must address relatively quickly once notified of an employee's resignation, then the actual transition process, and lastly how to leave the departing employee with a positive impression and experience.

Initial Considerations

(a) *Notifying Staff* – Management must decide when and how to notify the staff of news of departing employees. It should be a priority of management to mitigate harm to staff morale or concerns regarding workload capacity in response to this news.

(b) *Whether They Can Remain in Their Positions* – While most employers have certain requirements for providing appropriate notice by employees of their resignations, usually at least a couple of weeks, there are circumstances in which employees cannot be allowed to continue in their positions until their stated resignation dates. There are considerations employers may need to assess that may require that the employee's employment be ended immediately once notified of certain information, such as who an employee intends to work for following their departure, which may create a conflict of interest.

(c) *Resignation Letter* – Employers should get departing employees' resignations in writing. The resignation letters should explicitly state the reasons for their resignations and the effective dates of their resignations. A resignation letter can help the organization protect itself against future claims, such as a lawsuit for wrongful termination or constructive discharge, as well as protect against unemployment claims.

Transition/Succession Planning

(a) *Exit Interview* – Understanding why an employee left can be valuable information for an organization (e.g., lack of opportunities, not challenged, a problem supervisor, etc.). Exit interviews are excellent opportunities to get valuable, candid, unbiased feedback from individuals internal to the organization because there generally is no fear of reprisal for being critical. If possible, exit interviews should be conducted by a leader or manager that the person knows and feels comfortable with, to help get genuine feedback. If the interview cannot be done in person, which is preferred, it can be completed via an online survey.

(b) *Knowledge Transfer* – An obvious concern employers must address is who will handle the departing employee's responsibilities. If the departing employee had been with the organization for a long time or has specialized knowledge, it is important to make sure that management understands the position and all that it is accountable for. Be sure to ask departing employees if there is anything they do that they anticipate others may not know how to complete or if there are tasks that may fall outside of their job descriptions. Some positions grow over the years and it is important to understand whether that is the case so that the replacement is set up for success.

(c) *Replacement* – Regardless of how long departing employees stay until their effective resignation dates, plans for their succession should be initiated immediately. Any opportunity for departing employees to conduct crossover training with their replacements should be taken. Plans to hire replacements or backfill should be communicated with staff. This will help with morale and anxiousness over future workload concerns. It is also a best practice to ask departing employees if they have any recommendations for their replacements.

Positive Departure

(a) *Pleasant Farewell* – Employers should aim to make the resignation and departure process a pleasant and respectful experience for departing employees, especially those leaving in good standing. Although they may be viewed as no longer adding value to the organization, how the employer treats resigning employees throughout this process can be viewed by other employees as a reflection of the employer's genuine feelings and care for its employees. Additionally, a departing employee is in many ways still an ambassador of the organization, and having former employees disparaging their old employer can be bad for business.

(b) *Reference Letter* – One way employers can demonstrate to their departing employees that they value their contributions and that they support them, despite their moving on, is to offer to write them positive reference letters. This should only be done if genuine praise can be given. It is better for an employer to indicate they will not be a negative reference if a prospective employer reaches out, than agreeing to write a mediocre reference letter or one the employer doesn't feel is a complete reflection of the individual's work.

(c) *Eligibility for Rehire* – A simple way to express appreciation for departing employees who are leaving in good standing is to let them know that they are eligible to come back, if they decide to do so. This may not be a guarantee for the same position, but a statement that they can return into an open position can help end the employment relationship on a good note or set up a positive continued relationship.

(d) *Career Advice/Network* – Expressing a desire to connect the departing employee with other opportunities or career advice, even introductions to industry contacts, is a great way to help leave the employee with a positive impression.

Additional Information

- Information Regarding the Validity of Severance Agreements and Release of Claims – **EEOC**, "Understanding Waivers of Discrimination Claims in Employee Severance Agreements," https://www.eeoc.gov/policy/docs/qanda_severance-agreements.html.

Glossary

Americans with Disabilities Act (ADA). The act prohibits discrimination against people with disabilities in several areas, including employment, transportation, public accommodations, communications, and access to state and local government programs and services. As it relates to employment, Title I of the ADA protects the rights of both employees and job seekers.

Age Discrimination in Employment Act (ADEA). The act protects certain applicants and employees forty years of age and older from discrimination on the basis of age in hiring, promotion, discharge, compensation, or terms, conditions, or privileges of employment. The ADEA is enforced by the Equal Employment Opportunity Commission.

Deductions (Impermissible/Permissible). For any work performed during the workweek, employees must be paid their full salary amounts. Employers may not make deductions from exempt employees' pay for absences caused by the employer or by the operating requirements of the business. If the exempt employee is ready, willing and able to work, an employer cannot make deductions from the exempt employee's pay when no work is available.

Department of Labor (DOL). The federal agency charged with administering and overseeing various federal labor laws that affect employment, including wages, overtime protections, and workers' rights, among other things.

Disparate Treatment (Discrimination). A form of discrimination in which complainants allege that they are treated different from similarly situated employees because of their protected class (i.e., race, religion, gender, national origin, color, etc.).

Drug Free Workplace Act. This act requires, as a precondition of receiving a contract or grant from a federal agency of $100,000 or more, that the federal contractor or grantee agree to provide a drug-free workplace.

Equal Employment Opportunity Commission (EEOC). An independent federal agency that promotes equal opportunity in employment through administrative and judicial enforcement of the federal civil rights laws and through education and technical assistance.

Exempt Employee. One who is not entitled to the minimum wage or overtime pay protections of the FLSA.

Fair Labor Standards Act (FLSA). The act establishes minimum wage, overtime pay, recordkeeping, and youth employment standards affecting employees in the private sector and in federal, state, and local governments.

Family and Medical Leave Act (FMLA). The act entitles eligible employees of covered employers to take unpaid, job-protected leave for specified family and medical reasons with continuation of group health insurance coverage under the same terms and conditions as if the employee had not taken leave.

Job Description. The formal summary of employees' responsibilities associated with a particular position.

Noncompete Agreement. An agreement that prevents a separating employee from competing with the employer or working for a competitor of the employer within a limited geographical scope and for a period of time.

Nondisclosure Agreement/Confidentiality Agreement. An agreement that limits employees' use of trade secrets or other confidential information during and after their periods of employment.

Nonexempt Employee. One who is entitled to the minimum wage and overtime pay protections of the FLSA.

Non-Solicitation Agreement. An agreement that precludes an employee from soliciting clients of the employer for a period of time after separation.

Non-Recruitment Agreement. This agreement prevents a prior employee from recruiting other current employees of the employer for a period of time after termination.

Post-Employment Agreement. Also known as a restrictive covenant, this is a contract providing that the employee agrees not to engage in specific actions once their employment has concluded, for a specified amount of time, such as noncompetes, nonsolicits, and nondisclosure agreements.

Progressive Discipline. The process of issuing discipline that increases in severity after employees fail to correct their actions and for repeat offenses.

Title VII. The section of the Civil Rights Act that prohibits discrimination in hiring, promotion, discharge, pay, fringe benefits, job training, classification, referral, and other aspects of employment, on the basis of race, color, religion, sex, or national origin.

Notes

1. Insureon, "Majority of Small Businesses Lack Basic Business Bankruptcy Protection," November 30, 2017, https://www.insureon.com/blog/small-business-bankruptcy-poll.
2. Dave Kenney, "4 Onboarding Tips to Reduce Turnover," Efficient Hire, December 4, 2018, https://www.efficienthire.com/4-onboarding-tips-reduce-turnover/.
3. Alex Graaff, "How to Write a Lawsuit-Proof Job Description," NFIB, June 5, 2018, https://www.nfib.com/content/resources/staffing/how-to-write-a-lawsuit-proof-job-description/.
4. Jaime Lizotte, "True Stories: Hiring Mistakes That Can Turn into Costly Discrimination Claims," SCORE, January 24, 2019, https://www.score.org/blog/true-stories-hiring-mistakes-can-turn-costly-discrimination-claims.
5. National Conference of State Legislatures, "State Social Media Privacy Laws," May 22, 2019, http://www.ncsl.org/research/telecommunications-and-information-technology/state-laws-prohibiting-access-to-social-media-usernames-and-passwords.aspx.
6. US Equal Employment Opportunity Commission, "Background Checks: What Employers Need to Know," https://www.eeoc.gov/eeoc/publications/background_checks_employers.cfm.

7. Lisa Guerin, "State Laws on Use of Arrests and Convictions in Employment," NOLO, https://www.nolo.com/legal-encyclopedia/state-laws-use-arrests-convictions-employ ment.html.
8. EEOC, "Enforcement Guidance: Preemployment Disability-Related Questions and Medical Examinations," https://www.eeoc.gov/policy/docs/preemp.html.
9. Ibid.
10. The National Council for Voluntary Organisations, "How to Avoid Illegal or Inappropriate Interview Questions," https://knowhow.ncvo.org.uk/how-to/how-to-avoid-illegal-or-innapropriate-interview-questions.
11. Jamie Maggard and John Vering, "Overreaching Covenants Not to Compete Under Attack from All Sides," American Bar Association, December 26, 2018, https://www.americanbar.org/groups/litigation/committees/business-torts-unfair-competition/practice/2018/over-reaching-covenants-not-to-compete/.
12. Fox Rothschild, "National Survey on Restrictive Covenants," July 2017, https://www.foxrothschild.com/publications/national-survey-on-restrictive-covenants-in-employment/.
13. Administrative Office of the US Courts, "Table C-2—U.S. District Courts – Civil Judicial Business (September 30, 1997)," https://www.uscourts.gov/statistics-reports/caseload-statistics-data-tables.
14. Administrative Office of the US Courts, "Table C-2—U.S. District Courts – Civil Statistical Tables for the Federal Judiciary (December 31, 2018)," https://www.uscourts.gov/statistics-reports/caseload-statistics-data-tables.

15. US Department of Labor, Wage and Hour Division, "Wage and Hour Division Data," https://www.dol.gov/agencies/whd/data.
16. DOL, "Am I Covered by the FLSA?," elaws—Fair Labor Standards Act Advisor, https://webapps.dol.gov/elaws/whd/flsa/scope/screen10.asp.
17. DOL, Wage and Hour Division, "U.S. Department of Labor Recovers $3.2 Million in Back Wages, Damages, and Penalties from Portland, Oregon, Courier Service," news release no. 18-1721-SAN, November 27, 2018, https://www.dol.gov/newsroom/releases/whd/whd20181127-0.
18. Fair Labor Standards Act, 29 U.S.C. 203(e), (g).
19. DOL, Wage and Hour Division, "Fact Sheet 13: Employment Relationship Under the Fair Labor Standards Act," July, 2008, https://www.dol.gov/whd/regs/compliance/whdfs13.htm.
20. Ibid; and DOL, "Independent Contractors," elaws—Fair Labor Standards Act Advisor, https://webapps.dol.gov/elaws/whd/flsa/docs/contractors.asp.
21. Kate Tornone, "New California Independent Contractor Test Assumes Workers Are Employees," HR Dive, May 1, 2018, https://www.hrdive.com/news/new-california-independent-contractor-test-assumes-workers-are-employees/522497/.
22. TSheets, "The Top 10 Most Expensive FLSA Overtime Lawsuits of 2017," December 1, 2017, https://blog.tsheets.com/2017/business-help/most-expensive-flsa-overtime-lawsuits-2017; and Megan Rose Dickey, "Zenefits will

Pay $3.4 Million in Unpaid Overtime to 743 Employees," TechCrunch, June 20, 2017, https://techcrunch.com/2017/06/20/zenefits-will-pay-3-4-million-in-unpaid-overtime-to-743-employees/.

23. DOL, "Exemptions," elaws—Fair Labor Standards Act Advisor, https://webapps.dol.gov/elaws/whd/flsa/screen75.asp.
24. FLSA, 29 U.S.C. 213.
25. DOL, Wage and Hour Division, "Defining and Delimiting the Exemptions for Executive, Administrative, Professional, Outside Sales and Computer Employees," 29 C.F.R. § 541.602(a)—Salary, https://www.law.cornell.edu/cfr/text/29/541.602. See also DOL, "Glossary: salary," elaws – FLSA Overtime Security Advisor, https://webapps.dol.gov/elaws/whd/flsa/overtime/glossary.htm?wd=salary.
26. DOL, "Glossary: fee basis," elaws – FLSA Overtime Security Advisor, https://webapps.dol.gov/elaws/whd/flsa/overtime/glossary.htm?wd=fee_basis.
27. "Defining and Delimiting the Exemptions for Executive, Administrative, Professional, Computer and Outside Sales Employees," Code of Federal Regulations, 29 C.F.R. § 541.600-607, https://www.ecfr.gov/cgi-bin/text-idx?c=ecfr&sid=48d6ee3b99d3b3a97b1bf189e1757786&rgn=div5&view=text&node=29:3.1.1.1.23&idno=2.
28. Amount of Salary Required, 29 C.F.R. § 541, Amendments, 84 FR 51306, September 27, 2019, https://www.ecfr.gov/cgi-bin/text-idx?SID=8d1ac6a0599099b6a7635caa5c9e468f&mc=true&node=20190927y1.15.

29. DOL, "Compensation Requirements – Deductions," elaws—FLSA Overtime Security Advisor, https://webapps.dol.gov/elaws/whd/flsa/overtime/cr4.htm#2.
30. DOL, "Glossary," elaws—FLSA Overtime Security Advisor, https://webapps.dol.gov/elaws/whd/flsa/overtime/glossary. htm?wd=primary_duty.
31. Ibid.
32. FLSA, 29 U.S.C. 213, C.F.R. § 541.700(a). See also DOL, "Glossary: primary duty," elaws – FLSA Overtime Security Advisor, https://webapps.dol.gov/elaws/whd/flsa/overtime/glossary.htm?wd=primary_duty.
33. DOL, "Exemptions," elaws—Fair Labor Standards Act Advisor, https://webapps.dol.gov/elaws/whd/flsa/screen75.asp.
34. Pechman Law Group, "TGI Friday's Settles Wage Theft Case for $19.1 Million," WaiterPay.com, September 20, 2017, https://waiterpay.com/blog/tgi-fridays-settles-wage-theft-case-19-1-million.
35. FLSA, 29 U.S.C. 203(g).
36. DOL, "Break and Meal Periods," https://www.dol.gov/general/topic/workhours/breaks. See also DOL, "What does the Fair Labor Standards Act NOT Require?," elaws—Fair Labor Standards Act Advisor, https://webapps.dol.gov/elaws/whd/flsa/screen6.asp.
37. Anderson v. Mt. Clemens Pottery Co., 328 U.S. 680 (1946). See also FLSA, 29 U.S.C. 206 and 29 C.F.R. 785.7, https://www.dol.gov/whd/regs/compliance/wh131 2.pdf.
38. Ibid. See also DOL, Wage and Hour Division, "Fact Sheet 22: Hours Worked Under the Fair Labor Standards

Act," July 2008, https://www.dol.gov/whd/regs/compliance/whdfs22.htm.

39. Pierce, Britenae and Ryan Swanson, "FLSA Essentials: Practically Applying the Most Recent Legal Perspectives," lecture, National Business Institute, Human Resource Seattle, Washington, Law Boot Camp, March 2018.
40. Paula Hannaford-Agor and Nicole L. Waters, "Estimating the Cost of Civil Litigation," Court Statistics Project (National Center for State Courts) 20, no. 1(January 2013), http://www.courtstatistics.org/~/media/microsites/files/csp/data%20pdf/csph_online2.ashx?_ga=2.95132572.1899254267.1549199565-138526802.1547134723.
41. Gusto Editors, "Small Businesses and Employee Handbooks: Where Do You Stand?," Gusto, March 1, 2017, https://gusto.com/blog/people-management/small-businesses-employee-handbooks-stand-infographic. See also Felicia Sullivan and Kelly Spors, "The Ultimate Guide to Creating an Employee Handbook," Small Biz Ahead (The Hartford), March 2019, https://sba.thehartford.com/managing-employees/hiring/employee-handbook-guide/.
42. Kistler Tiffany Benefits, "Employee Handbooks: Common Legal Mistakes," http://ktbenefits.com/wp-content/uploads/2017/01/Employee-Handbooks-Common-Legal-Mistakes.pdf.
43. DOL, Wage and Hour Division, "Minimum Length of Meal Period Required Under State Law for Adult

Employees in Private Sector 1," January 1, 2019, https://www.dol.gov/whd/state/meal.htm.

44. Staschiak v. Certified Logistics, 2016-Ohio-897. See also Tracey Blair, "11th District: Employee Handbooks Can Be Implied Contracts," Akron Legal News, March 31, 2016, http://www.akronlegalnews.com/editorial/14933.
45. Garett Seivold, "Workplace Bullying and How to Avoid a $4.7 Million Lawsuit," Loss Prevention Magazine, June 4, 2019, https://losspreventionmedia.com/workplace-bullying-and-how-to-avoid-a-4-7-million-lawsuit/.
46. EEOC, "Charge Statistics (Charges filed with EEOC): FY 1997 Through FY 2017," https://www.eeoc.gov/eeoc/statistics/enforcement/charges.cfm.
47. Workplace Bullying Institute, "The WBI Definition of Workplace Bullying," https://www.workplacebullying.org/individuals/problem/definition/.
48. WBI, "Healthy Workplace Bill," https://healthyworkplacebill.org/states/.
49. DOL, Occupational Safety and Health Administration, "Employer Responsibilities," https://www.osha.gov/as/opa/worker/employer-responsibility.html.

    See also the Ninth Circuit Court of Appeals in Nichols v. Azteca Restaurant Enterprises, Inc., 256 F.3d 864 (9th Cir. 2001), stating, "When an employer undertakes no remedy, or where the remedy does not end the current harassment and deter future harassment, liability attaches for both the past harassment and any future harassment."
50. EEOC, Title VII of the Civil Rights Act of 1964, § 2000e-2, § 703(a), https://www.eeoc.gov/laws/statutes/titlevii.

cfm. See also EEOC, "Harassment," https://www1.eeoc.gov//laws/types/harassment.cfm?renderforprint=1.

51. Ibid. See also NOLO, "Employment Discrimination in Your State," https://www.nolo.com/legal-encyclopedia/employment-discrimination-in-your-state-31017.html.
52. David Sparkman, "One in Seven Employees Don't Feel Safe at Work," EHS Today, Mar 22, 2019, https://www.ehstoday.com/safety-2014/one-seven-employees-don-t-feel-safe-work.
53. Burlington Industries, Inc. v. Ellerth, 118 S. Ct. 2257 (1998).
54. Vance v. Ball State University, 133 S. Ct. 2434 (2013).
55. EEOC, Title VII of the Civil Rights Act of 1964, 29 C.F.R. 1604.11(d) – Sexual Harassment. See also EEOC, "Enforcement Guidance on Vicarious Employer Liability for Unlawful Harassment by Supervisors," https://www.eeoc.gov/policy/docs/harassment.html.
56. Matvia v. Bald Head Island Management, Inc., 259 F.3d 261, 268 (4th Cir. 2001).
57. EEOC, "Enforcement Guidance on Vicarious Employer Liability for Unlawful Harassment by Supervisors," https://www.eeoc.gov/policy/docs/harassment.html.
58. EEOC, "Harassment Policy Tips," https://www.eeoc.gov/employers/smallbusiness/checklists/harassment_policy_tips.cfm.
59. EEOC, "Enforcement Guidance on Vicarious Employer Liability for Unlawful Harassment by Supervisors," section V(C)(1), https://www.eeoc.gov/policy/docs/harassment.html.
html.

60. Ibid.
61. Ibid. ["Harassment" has been changed to "incident" or "inappropriate behavior" throughout.]
62. Ibid.
63. Ibid.
64. Ibid.
65. Melissa Gonzalez Boyce, "7 Policies to Update in Your 2019 Employee Handbook," SHRM, January 15, 2019, https://www.shrm.org/resourcesandtools/legal-and-compliance/state-and-local-updates/pages/7-policies-to-update-in-your-2019-employee-handbook.aspx.
66. The Drug Free Workplace Act, 41 U.S.C. 81.
67. Americans with Disabilities Act, 29 C.F.R. 1630.14(b)(3) – Medical Examinations and Inquiries Specifically Permitted. See also EEOC, "Questions and Answers: Enforcement Guidance on Disability-Related Inquiries and Medical Examinations of Employees Under the Americans with Disabilities Act (ADA)," https://www.eeoc.gov/policy/docs/qanda-inquiries.html.
68. Paycor, "Pre-Employment Drug Testing Laws By State," May 29, 2019, https://www.paycor.com/resource-center/pre-employment-drug-testing-laws-by-state. See also American Civil Liberties Union, "State-by-State Workplace Drug Testing Laws," https://www.aclu.org/other/state-state-workplace-drug-testing-laws.
69. Lisa Guerin, "Laws on Employee Drug Testing," NOLO, https://www.nolo.com/legal-encyclopedia/free-books/employee-rights-book/chapter5-3.html.
70. Americans with Disabilities Act of 1990, 42 U.S.C. §

12114(a)—Illegal Use of Drugs and Alcohol, https://www.eeoc.gov/laws/statutes/ada.cfm.

71. NORML, "State Info," https://norml.org/states.
72. ADA, 29 C.F.R. 1630.14(b) – Medical Examinations and Inquiries Specifically Permitted.
73. Mobile Health Management Services, Inc., "What Are the Different Drug Panels?," https://www.mobilehealth.net/screening/drug-screening/5-panel/the-different-drug-panels/.
74. Ibid.
75. Daniel V. Johns, "Toward a More Modern Application of the 'Nexus to the Workplace' Test: Arbitral Considerations in Off-Duty Employee Misconduct Cases," Harvard Negotiation Law Review 23, no. 1 (Fall 2017): 1-28, https://www.hnlr.org/wp-content/uploads/sites/22/HNLR-Johns.pdf.
76. National Conference of State Legislatures, "State Social Media Privacy Laws," May 22, 2019, http://www.ncsl.org/research/telecommunications-and-information-technology-state-laws-prohibiting-access-to-social-media-usernames-and-passwords.aspx.
77. Garett Seivold, "Workplace Bullying and How to Avoid a $4.7 Million Lawsuit," June 4, 2019, https://losspreventionmedia.com/workplace-bullying-and-how-to-avoid-a-4-7-million-lawsuit/.
78. David A. Dilts and James S. Moore, "Do Arbitrators Use Just Cause Standards in Deciding Discharge and Discipline Cases? A Test," Journal of Collective Negotiations 30, no. 3(September 2009): 245, 252.

79. Comply Right, "6 Tips for Properly Documenting Employee Behavior and Performance Issues," May 16, 2017, https://www.complyright.com/performance/6-tips-on-documenting-employee-behavior-and-performance-issues-properly.
80. SHRM, "How to Establish a Performance Improvement Plan," https://www.shrm.org/resourcesandtools/tools-and-samples/how-to-guides/pages/performanceimprovement-plan.aspx.
81. Lisa Nagele-Piazza and Allen Smith, "Should Employers Stay Friendly with Former Employees?," February 25, 2019, https://www.shrm.org/resourcesandtools/legal-and-compliance/employment-law/pages/friendly-former-employees.aspx.

About the Author

Ray Sugarman is the founder of Sugarman Consulting, PLLC, a consulting firm advising employers on how to navigate employment law and racial equity matters. Ray is a labor and employment law attorney, as well as a former representative for the City of Seattle's largest union. Prior to consulting and representing a union, he interned for one of California's top management-side labor and employment law firms, Paul, Plevin, Sullivan & Connaughton in San Diego, and later practiced for one of Washington's premier employee-side employment law firms, Vreeland Law. Ray is currently the Deputy Director of Operations for the Human Resource Division with the City of Seattle Finance and Administrative Services Department, overseeing all employee and labor relation matters for over 650 workers.

Ray's entire legal career has been spent identifying employer liability exposure in some capacity. In 2018, Ray was recognized as "a Rising Star in the field of employment law" by the American Institute of Legal Advocates, and designated a Top 40 Under 40 Attorney in the field of employment law for 2018 and again in 2019 by the Premier Lawyers of America. Ray's unique experience advocating for workers and advising employers has allowed him to become an established employment and labor law expert.

Made in the USA
Monee, IL
04 November 2026

67386133R10120